ISLAND MAIDENS

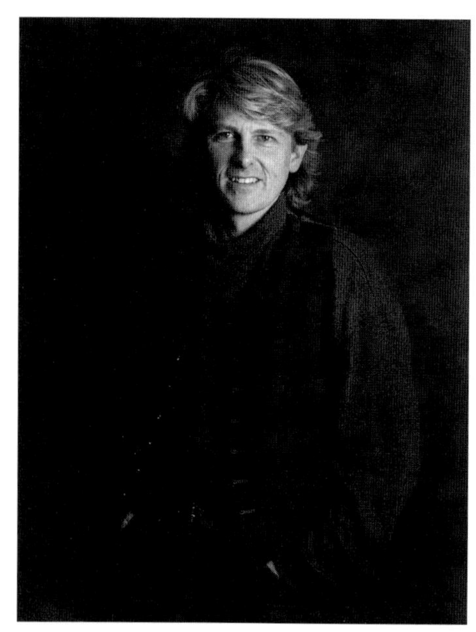

DAVID BETTS was born on the Isle of Wight – the 'island' of the title – and has lived there ever since. The island provides some beautiful and dramatic settings in which David enjoys creating images of mood and mystery. Although he took up photography in his teens, it is only in the last 10 years that he has been exploring the more creative aspects of the medium. A frequent lecturer and judge on the camera club circuit, David has had several of his images used commercially, including calendars and postcards. He works primarily in black and white, but often tones and tints prints for exhibition and private sale.

Photo of David Betts © John Sturt, 1995

ISLAND MAIDENS

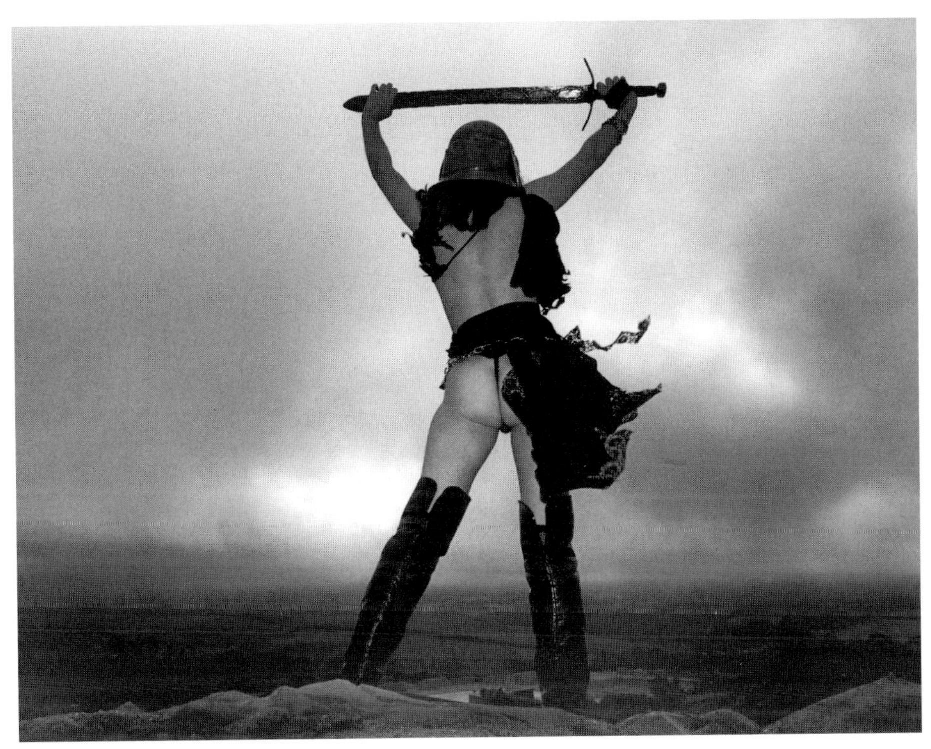

DAVID BETTS

A CREATIVE MONOCHROME PUBLICATION

ISLAND MAIDENS
the photography of DAVID BETTS

published in the UK by Creative Monochrome Limited
20 St Peters Road, Croydon, Surrey, CR0 1HD
telephone : 0181 686 3282; facsimile : 0181 681 0662
© Creative Monochrome Limited, 1995

British Library Cataloguing-in-Publication Data:
A catalogue record for this book is available from
the British Library

ISBN 1 873319 21 5

Printed in England by The Bath Press, Lower Bristol Road,
Bath, Avon, BA2 3BL

INTRODUCTION

I guess this book is the end of one dream, but at the same time I hope it may be the beginning of another.

To start at the beginning. I was born on the Isle of Wight, a beautiful island just off the coast of Hampshire. Even from an early age, I have always been fascinated with picture-taking. My father was a professional wedding and portrait photographer, so I grew up surrounded by photographic paraphernalia, although I was never directly encouraged to become involved in photography. I just seemed to drift into it as a second hobby at about the age of 17, with playing drums in a band being my first love.

This was the 'sixties and music was my main passion – the era of Jimi Hendrix and the Cream – and there I was living on the island which hosted the greatest pop festival in the world. And, from a photographic perspective, I missed it! How I dream of stepping back there now with camera in hand – I think I would get through quite a few rolls of film!

But I was, at least, giving my wonderful Zenit B some exercise during this period. I joined the local photographic society and, with much encouragement from a lovely lady called Doris Langford, I tried various photographic processes, including lith and solarisation – even resorting to dyeing my prints with clothes dye (as I said, this was the 'sixties!).

In my early 20s, both my parents died and this, combined with other factors, resulted in me losing interest in photography. Although I continued to take photographs, most of these were more record shots than creative gems. I came back to photography in my early thirties, since when I have become more and more engrossed in what seems to be becoming my lifetime passion.

Life tends to be driven by emotions and dreams, and this is certainly the case for me. This is why so many of my images have a sense of mystery or fantasy about them: I like to create pictures with mood and atmosphere. For me, much of the excitement in creating the images comes in the darkroom, when I am able to manipulate the prints to achieve the desired mood. I find that listening to music while working in the darkroom helps to generate the emotions which I can then try to convey into the prints.

I suppose I am a typical Gemini person with a dual personality, because I love the old-fashioned, soft and romantic images, harking back to the Victorians, and yet I also love the erotic pictures by people like Helmut Newton and Bob Carlos Clarke. So my work seems to cross in and out of these two main styles.

The photographs shown in this book span the last 10 years and have all been taken on the Isle of Wight. I would like to take this opportunity to say a big 'thank you' to all the girls who have given up their time to pose for me in sometimes rather bizarre states of undress and often in inhospitable weather. Particular thanks to Sally, without whom this portfolio would not have been possible.

Over the last two years I have been busily involved in trying to find outlets for my work, culminating in getting this book accepted by a publisher. Putting the work together for this book was a particular challenge as I normally tone and hand-tint my work, which was obviously not appropriate for a monochrome book. I hope that if this book is well received I will have the opportunity to share some of my toned and tinted images with an equally large audience.

I would never have reached the point of having this book published if it were not for the support and encouragement of my wife, Helen. She helped me survive the difficult years in my early twenties and it was her tolerance of my photographic obsession which has helped me to achieve this dream.

For the technically minded, I should add a few words about the equipment and materials I use. Many of the pictures in this book were taken on a fairly old Pentax, which has now been replaced with a Nikon, my favourite lens for which is a 20mm wide angle. I also now use a Bronica medium format camera, again favouring a wide angle (40mm in this case) lens. Like most photographers, my film stock has varied over the years, but I currently work mainly with Agfa film and paper. I also love using Infrared film for its dreamlike qualities, which is helpful in building mood and mystery: the stuff of dreams!

What of my dreams for the future? I want to continue to take pictures and wish for each image to be better than the last; but, above all, I hope that people will enjoy my work and want to see more.

PORTFOLIO

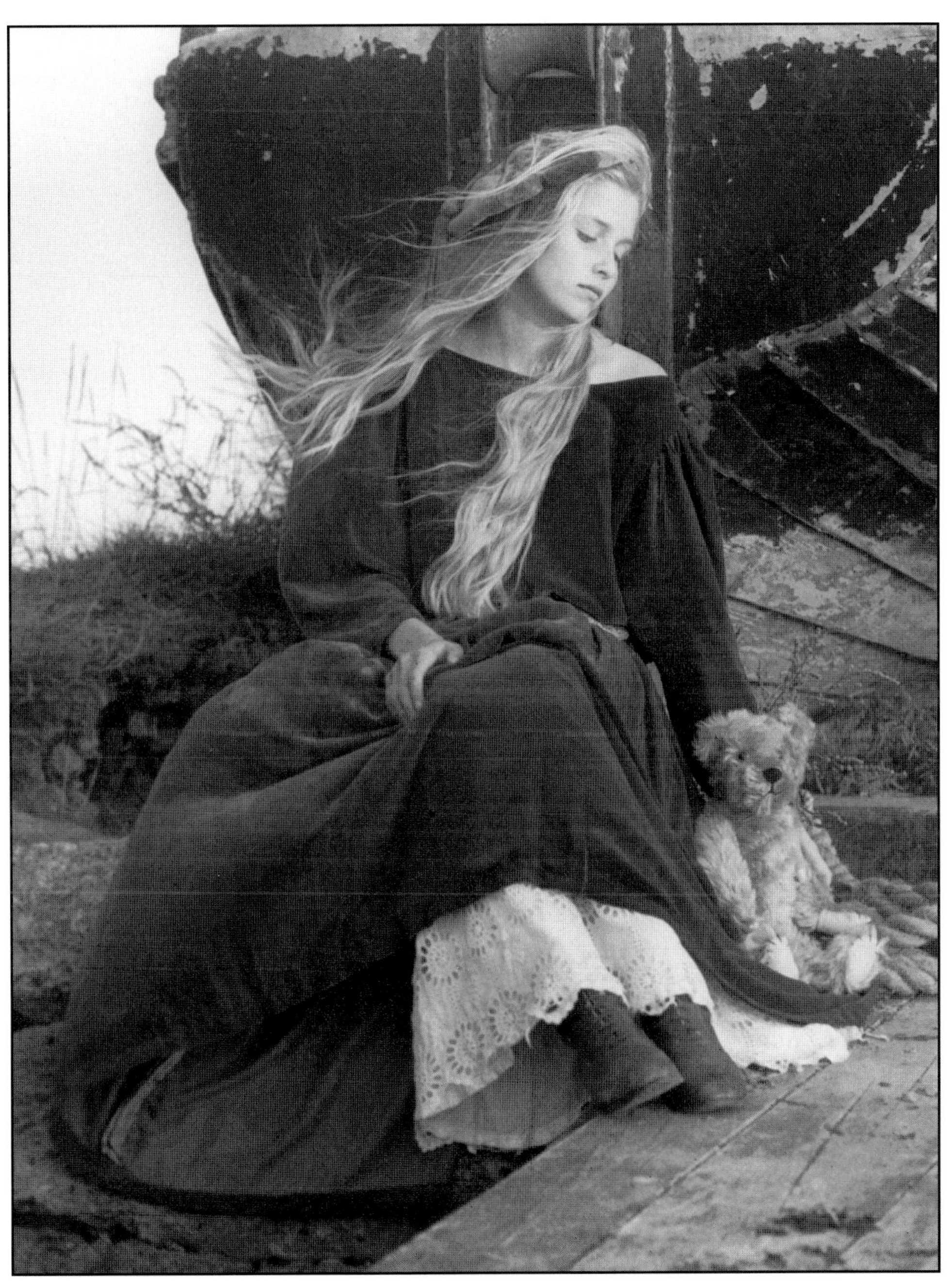

plate 1

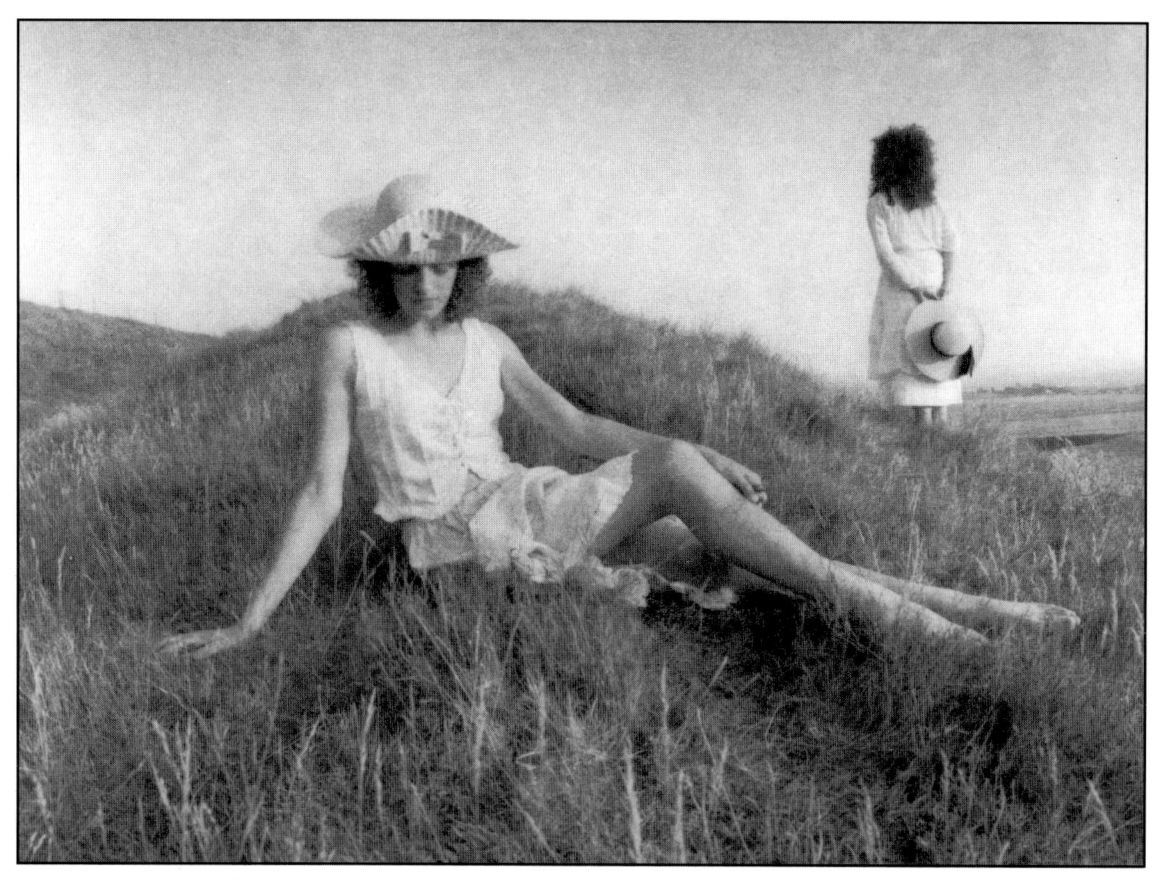

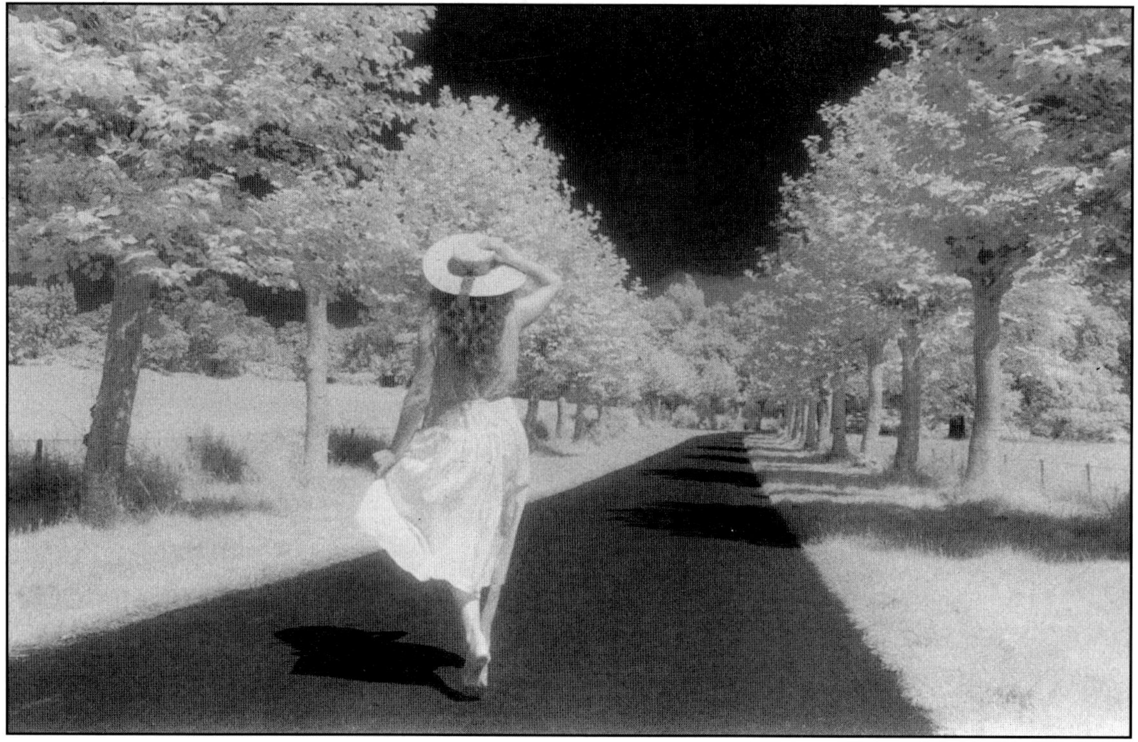

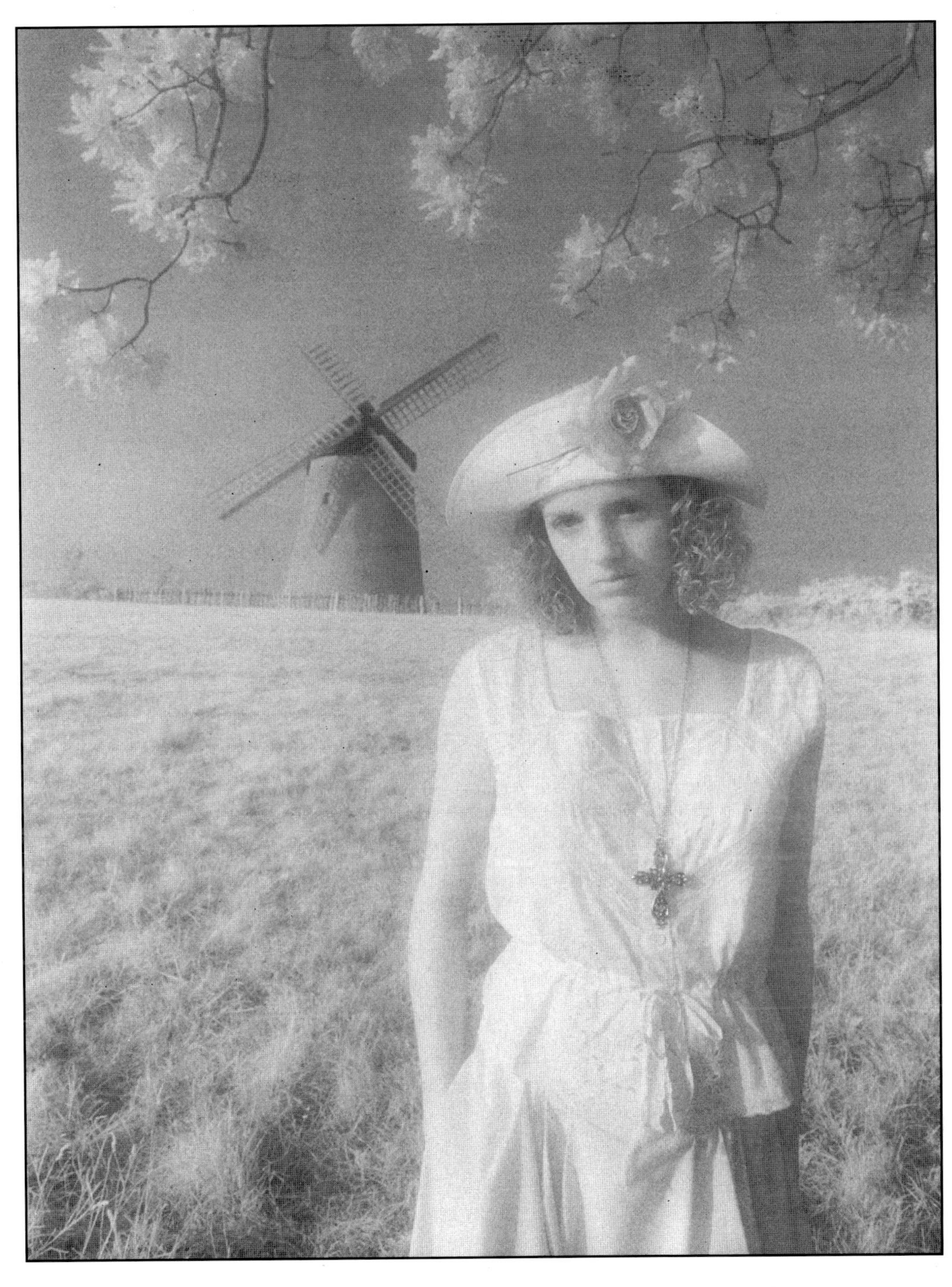

above: plate 4
opposite: plate 2 (top), plate 3 (below)

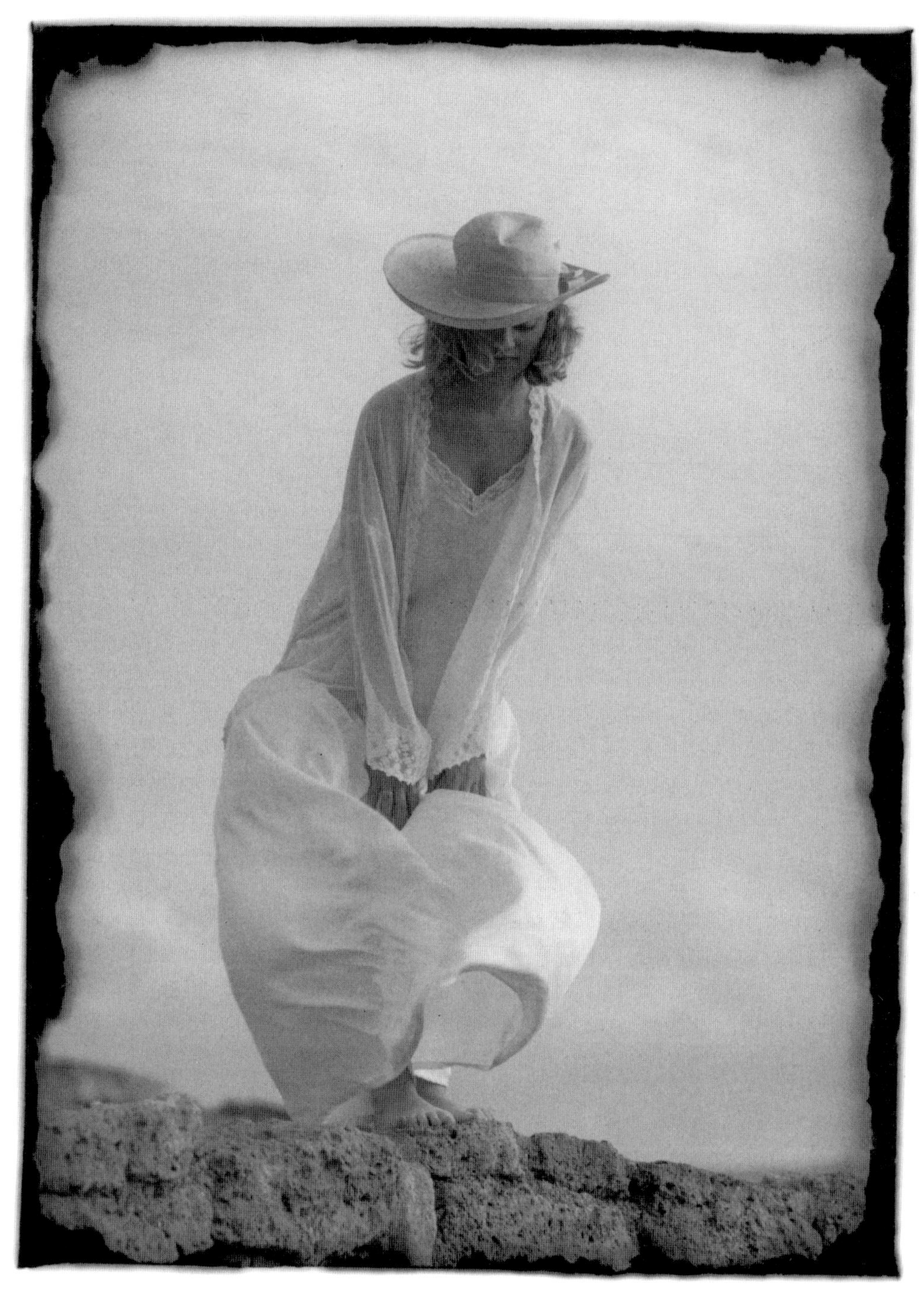

plate 5

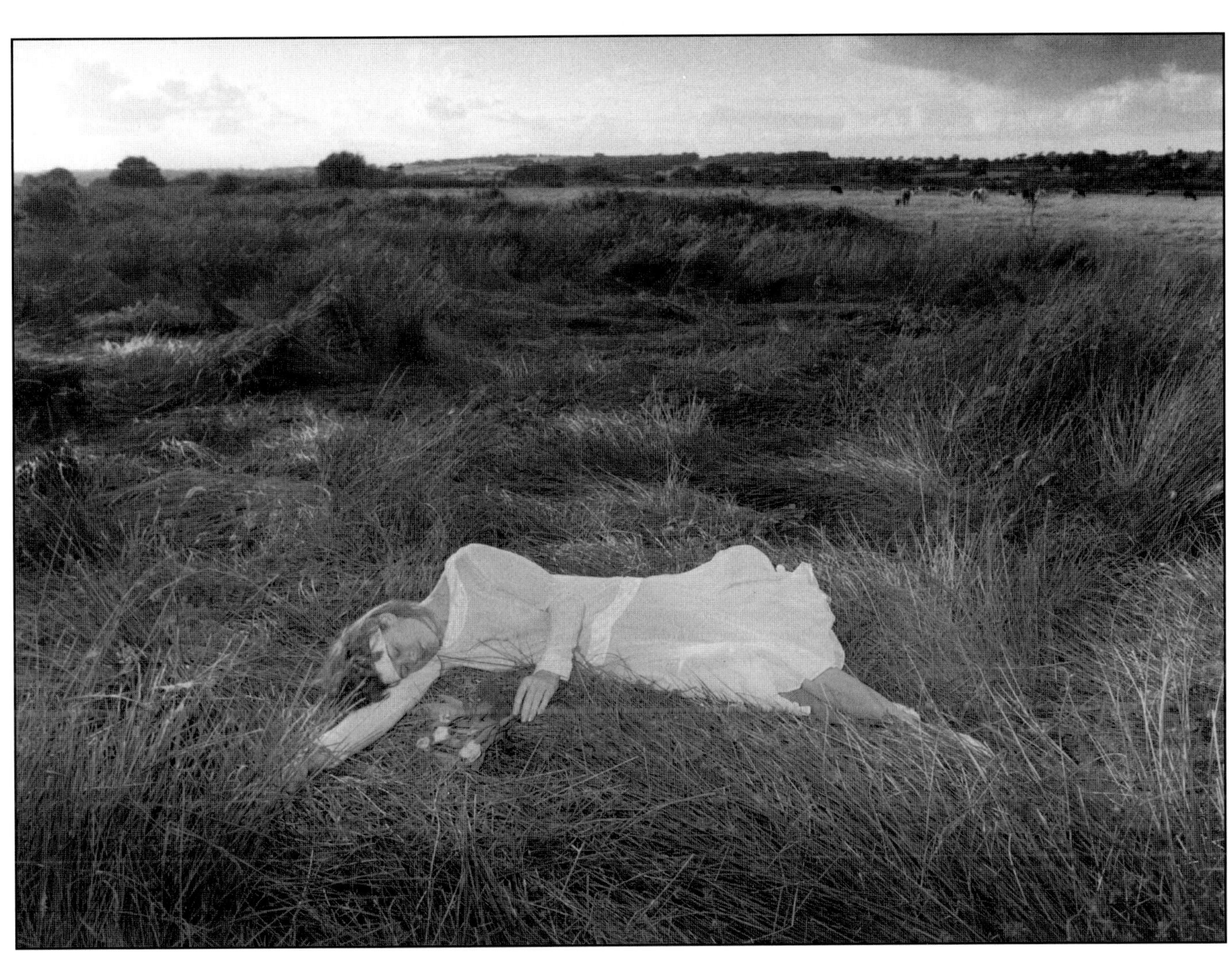

plate 6

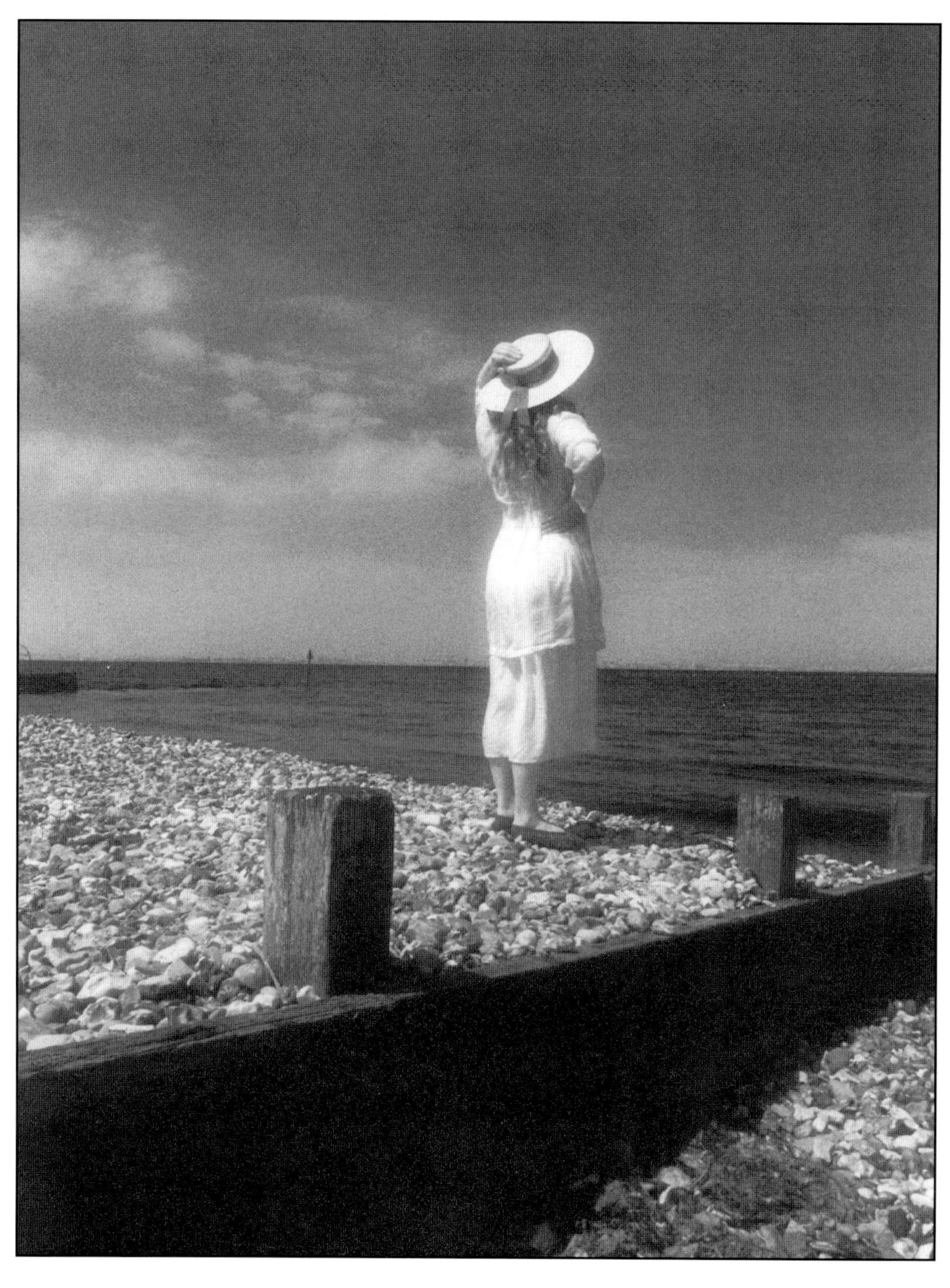

plate 7

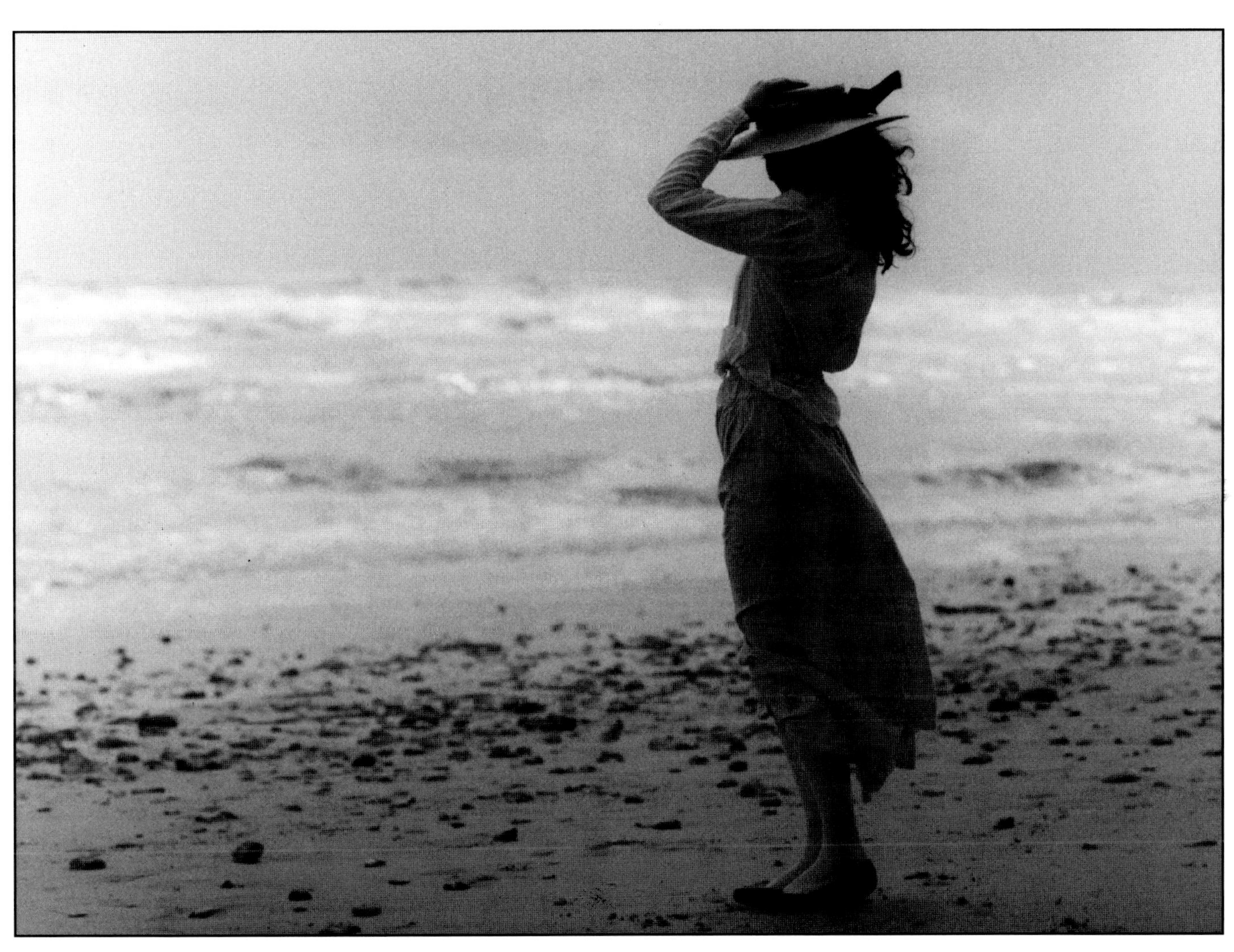

plate 8

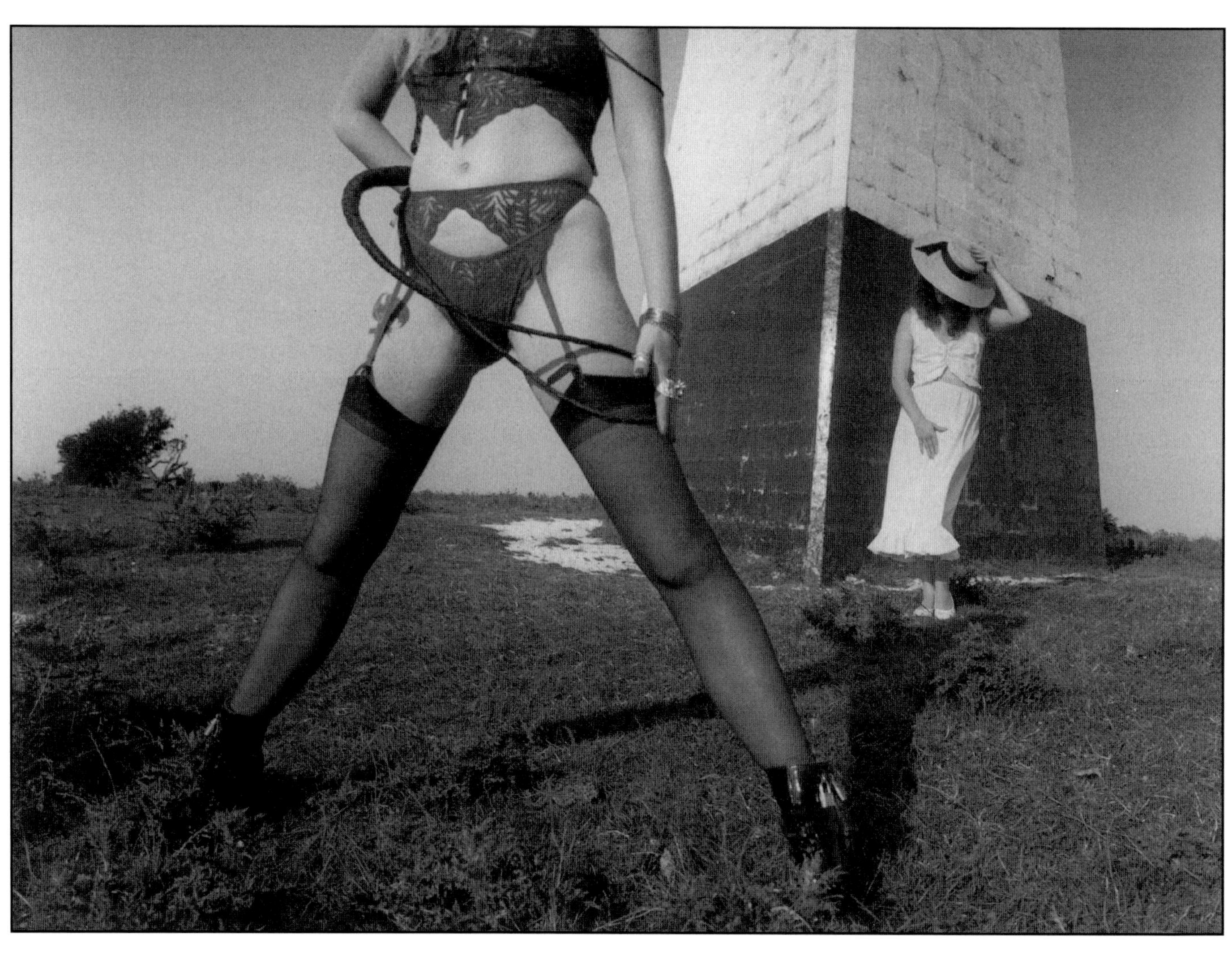

plate 9

14

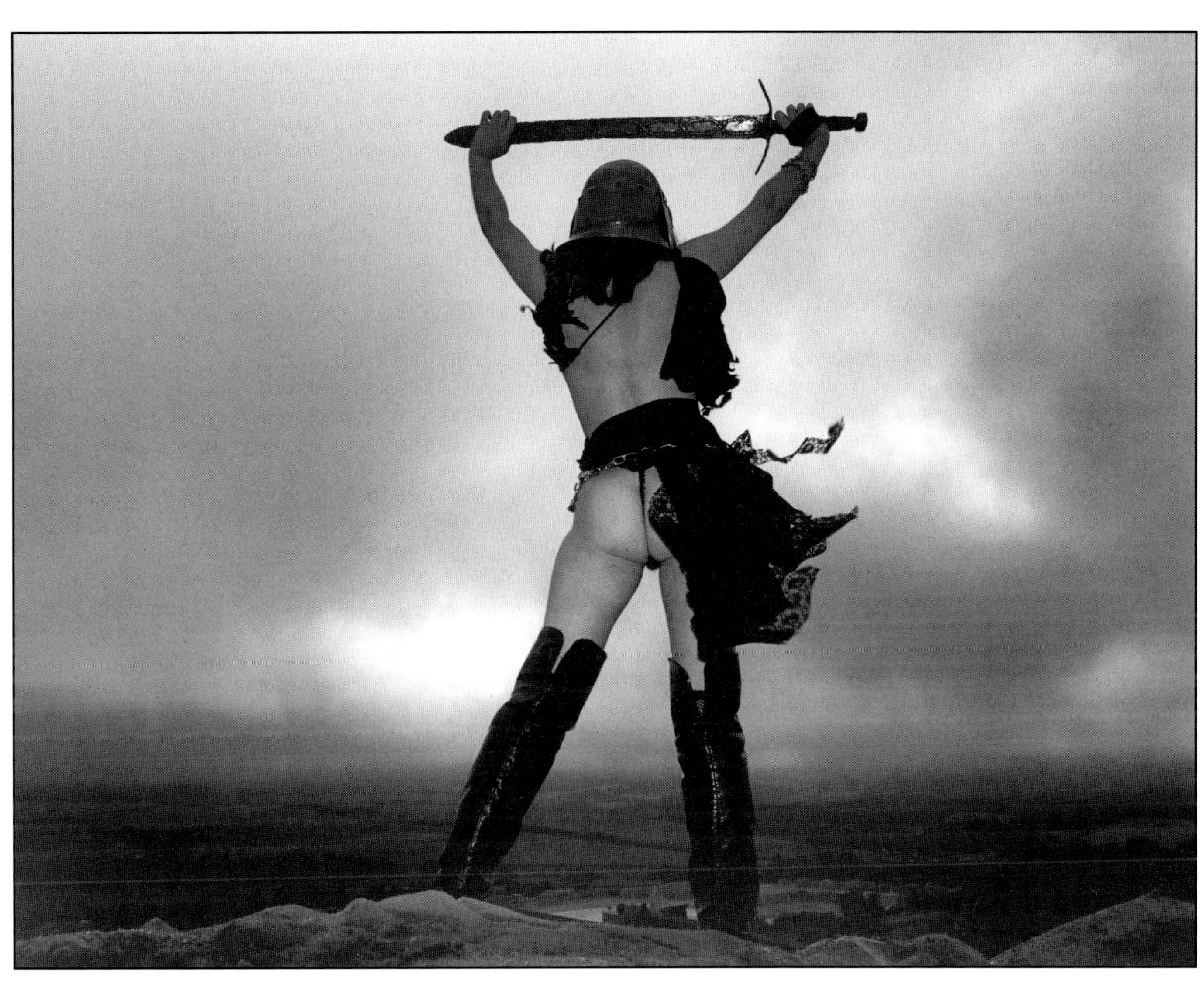

plate 10

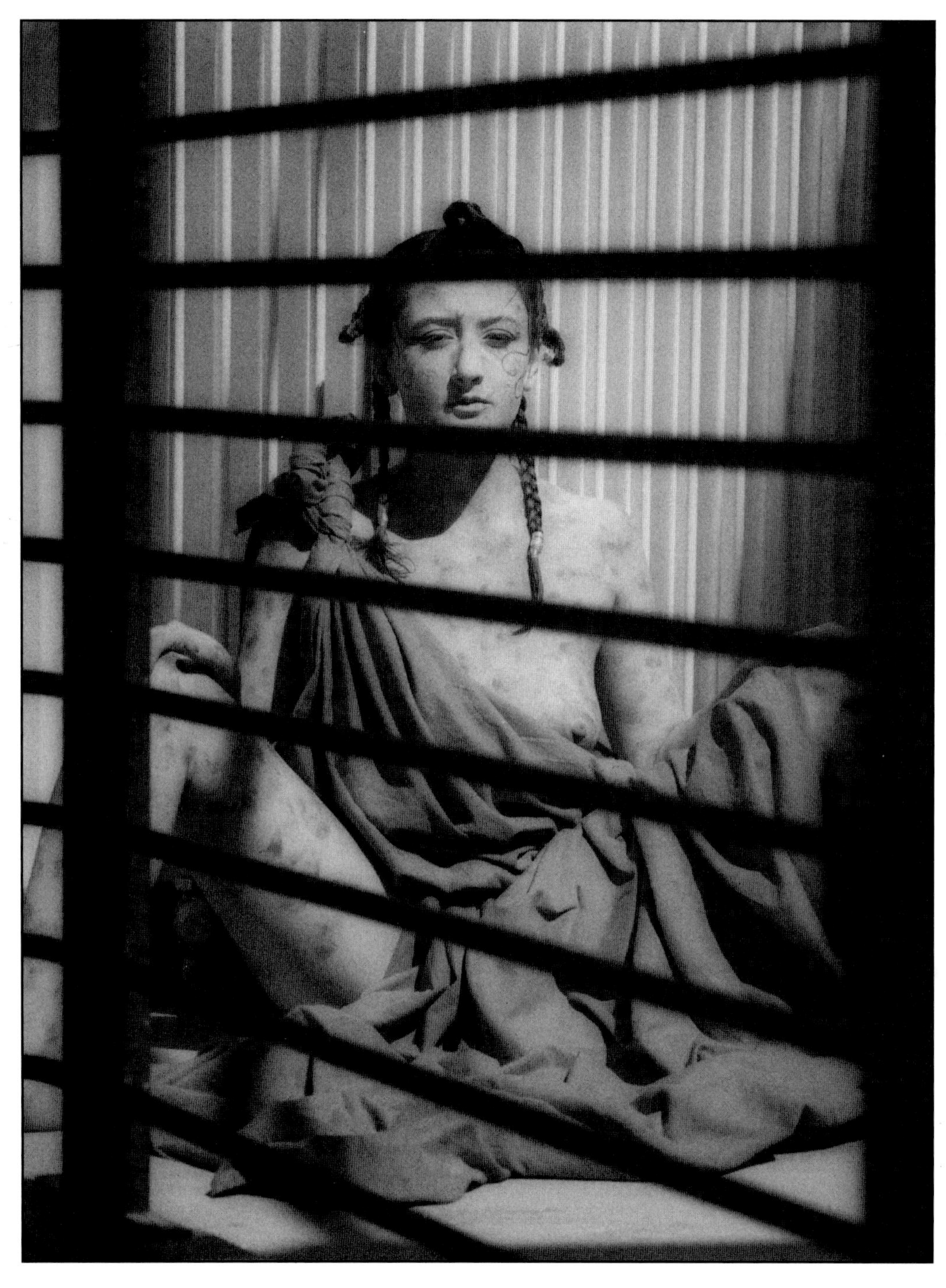

plate 11

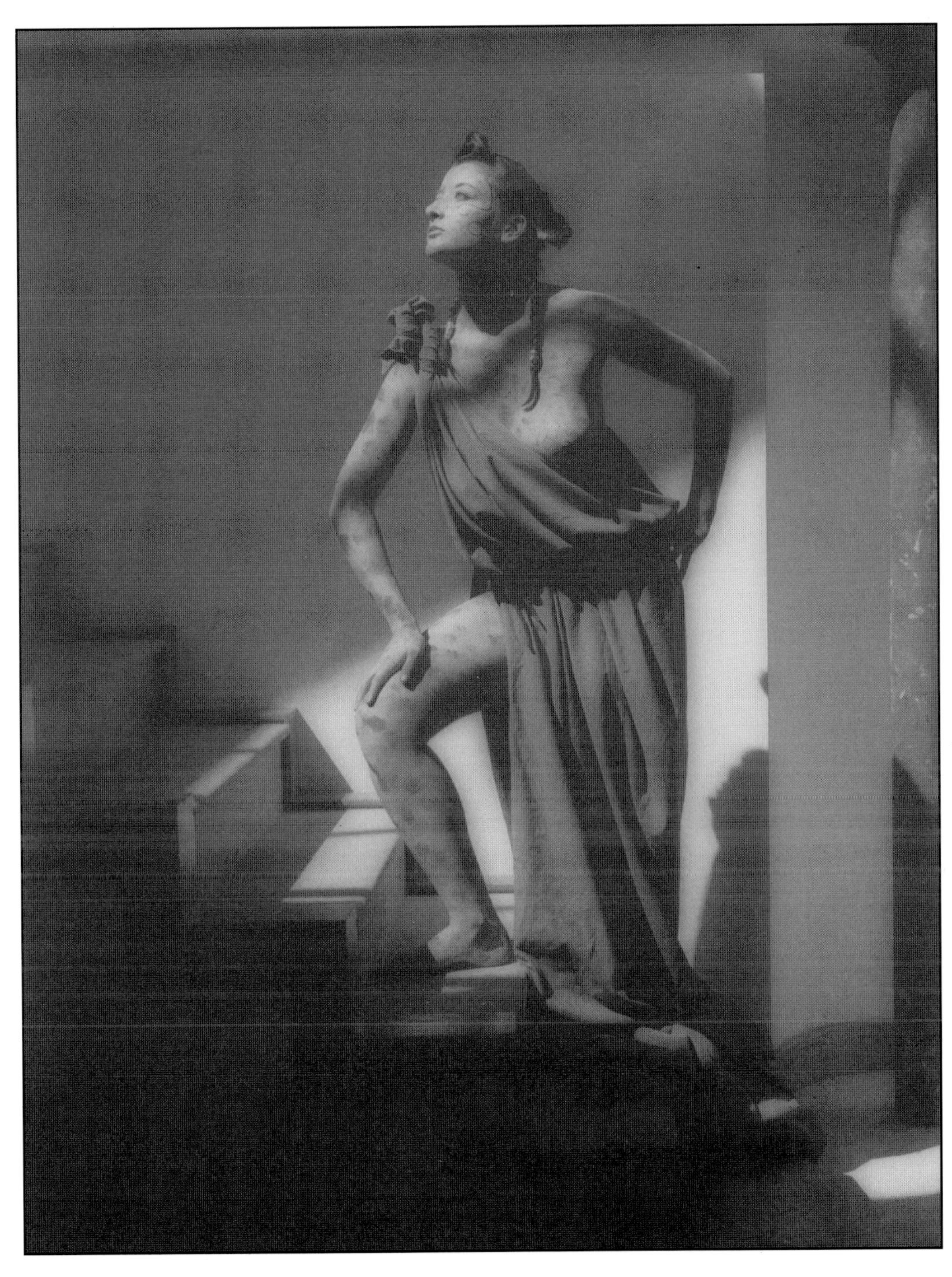

plate 12

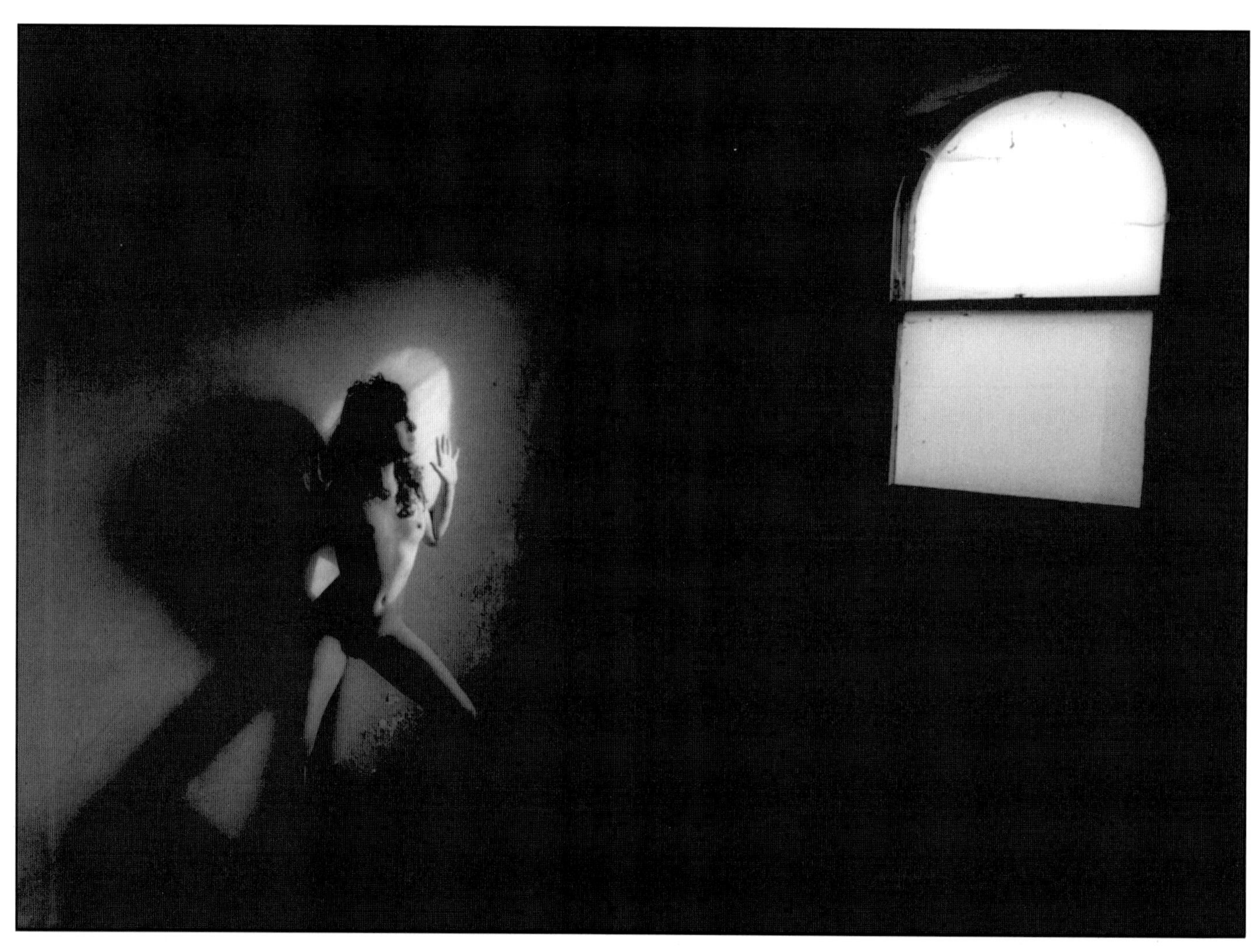

plate 13

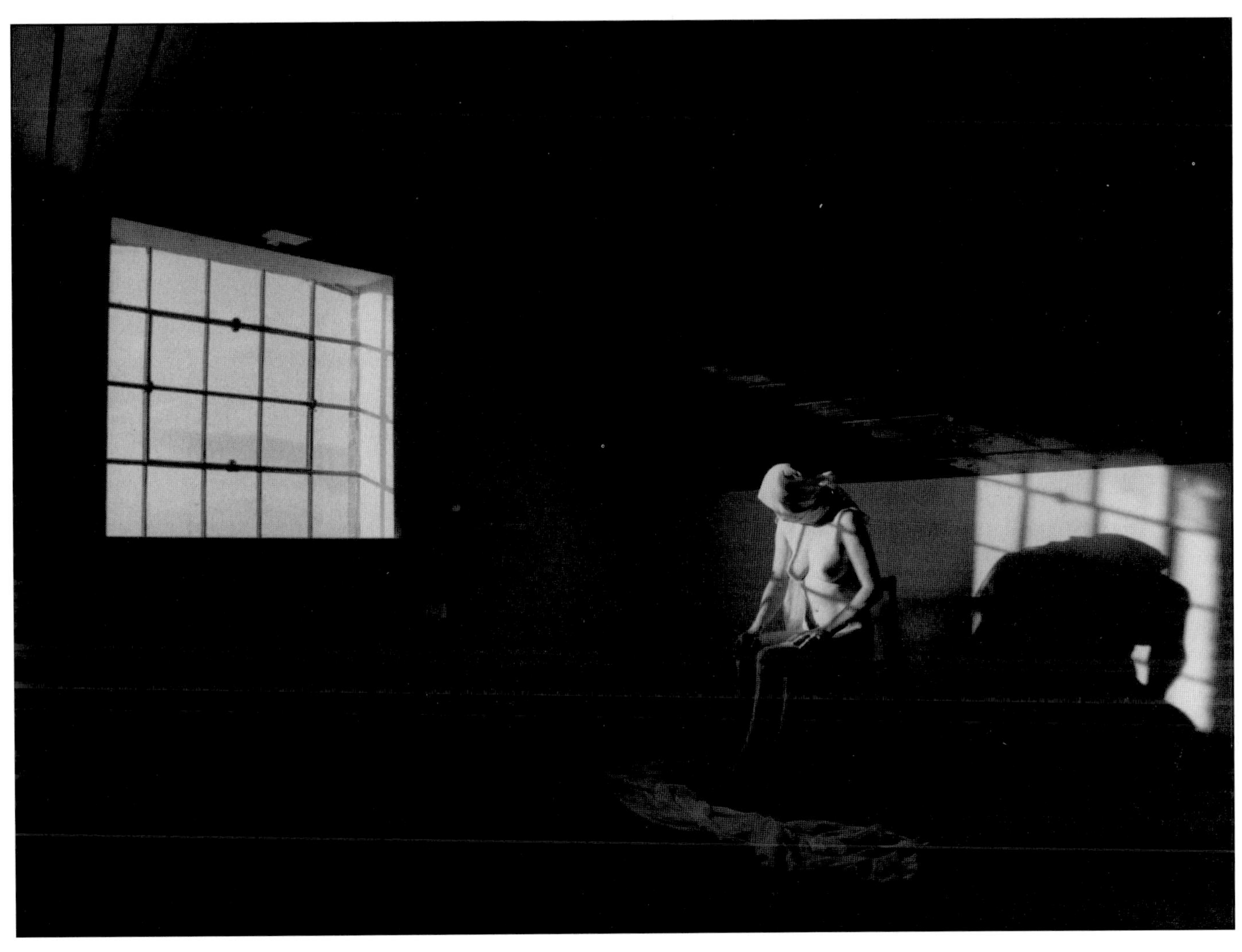

plate 14

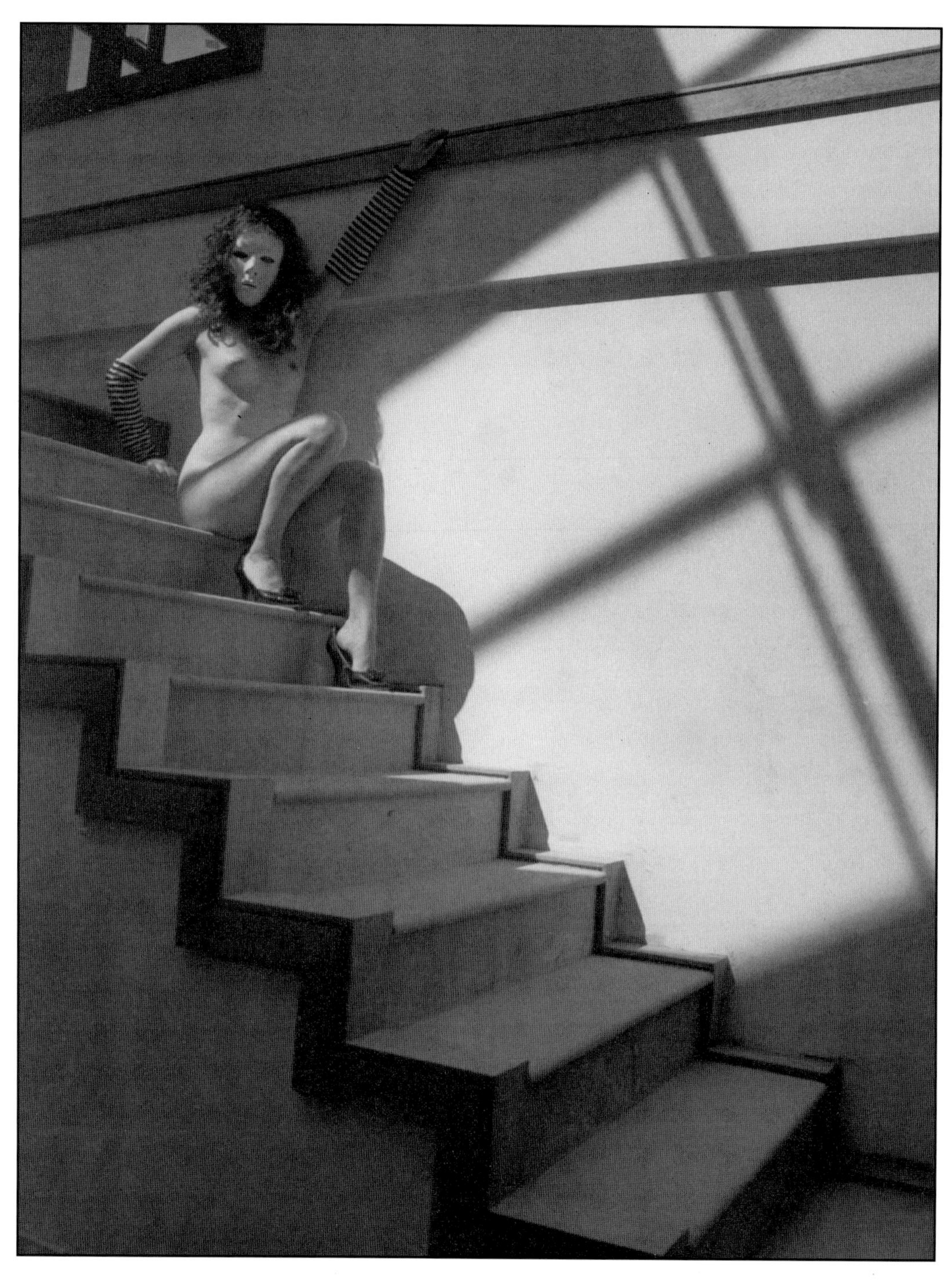

above: plate 15
opposite: plate 16 (top); plate 17 (below)

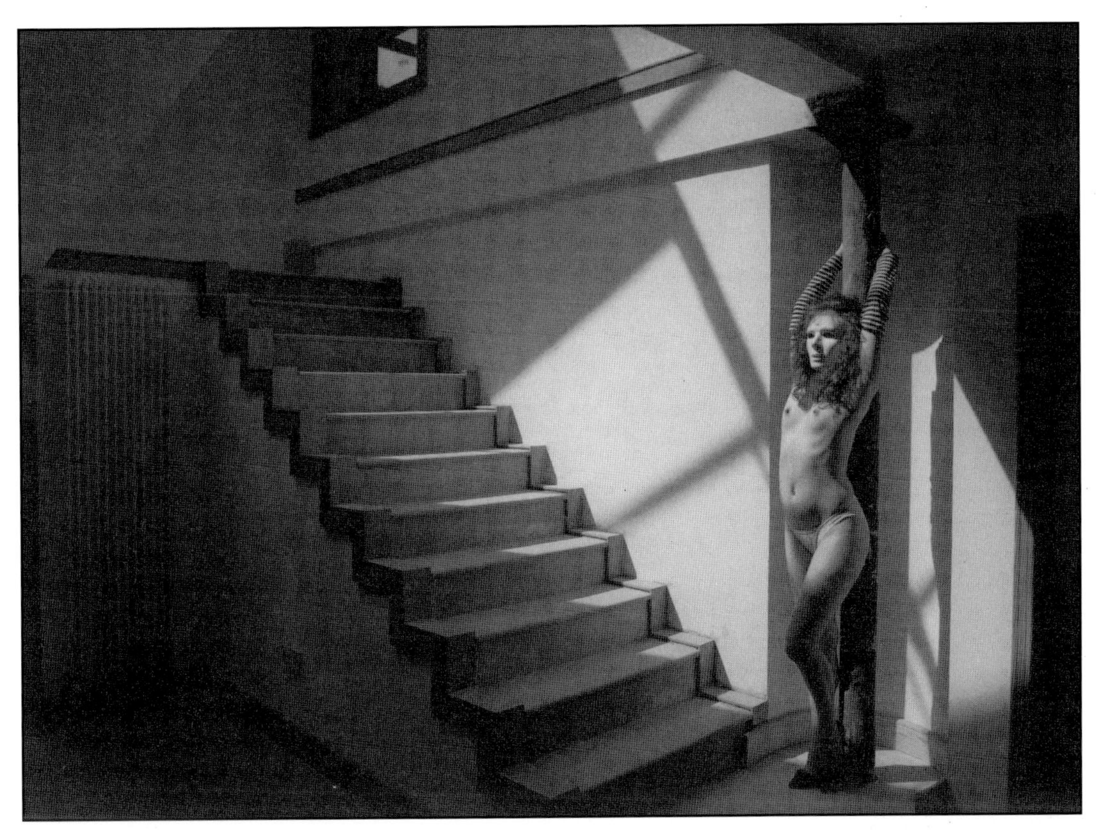

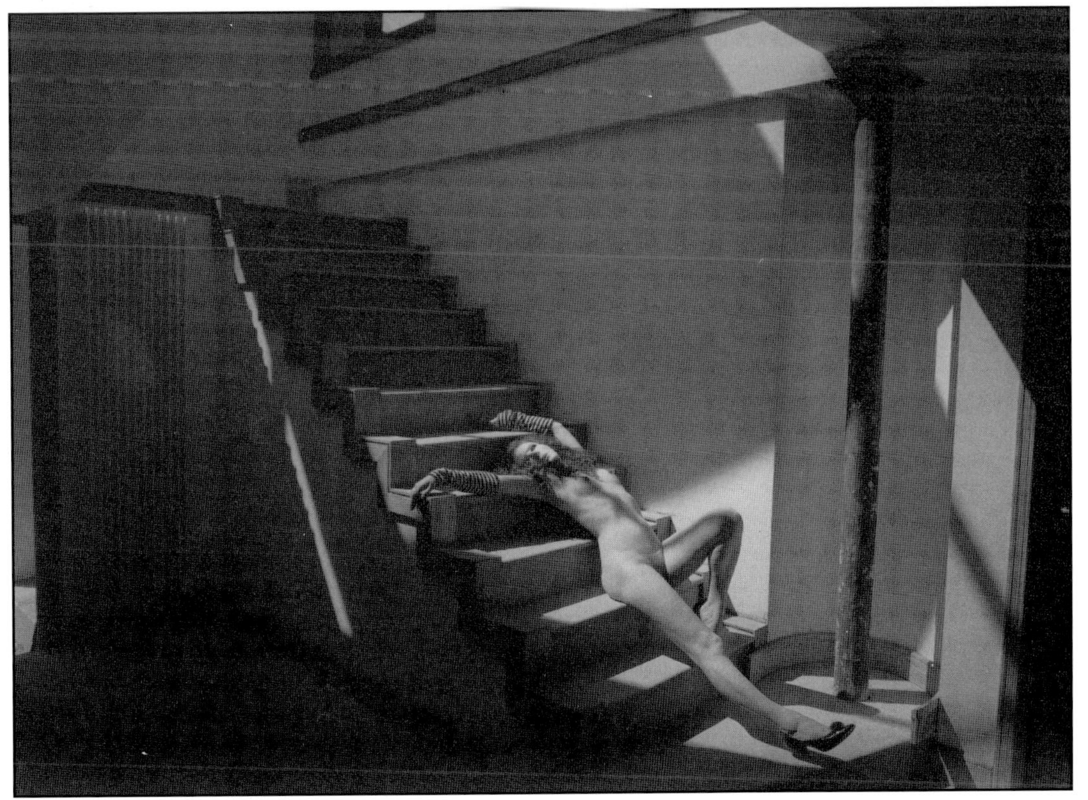

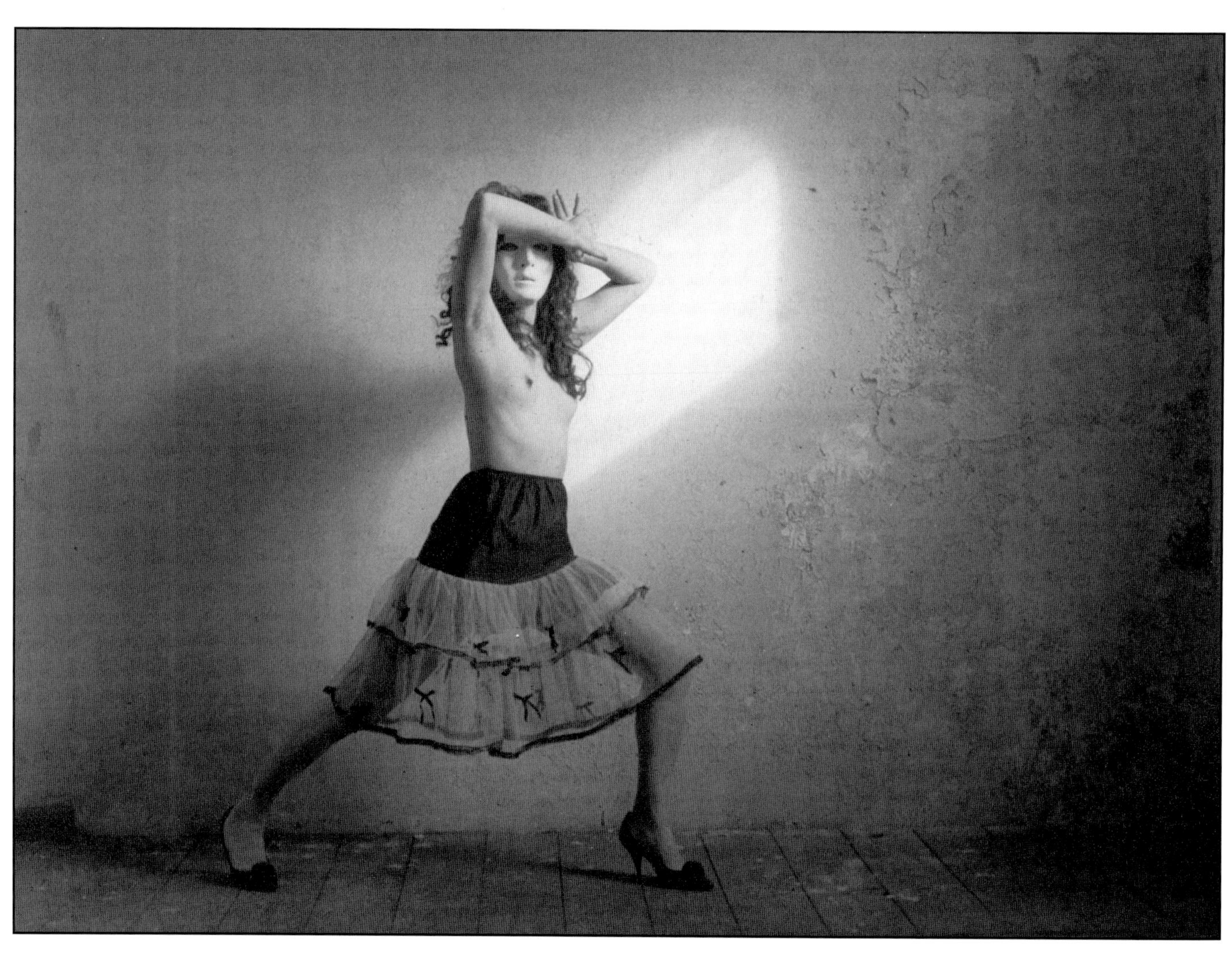

plate 18

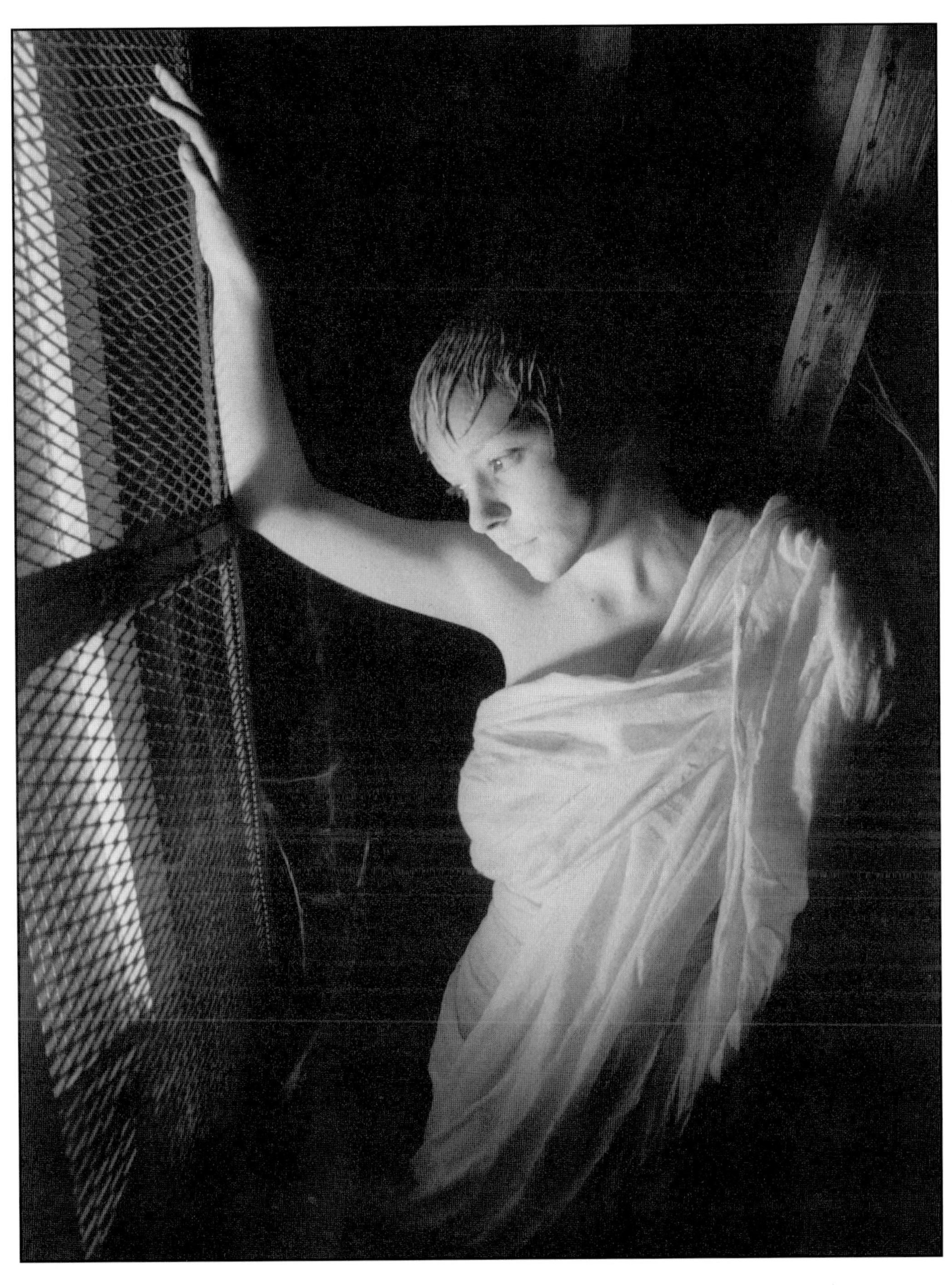

plate 19

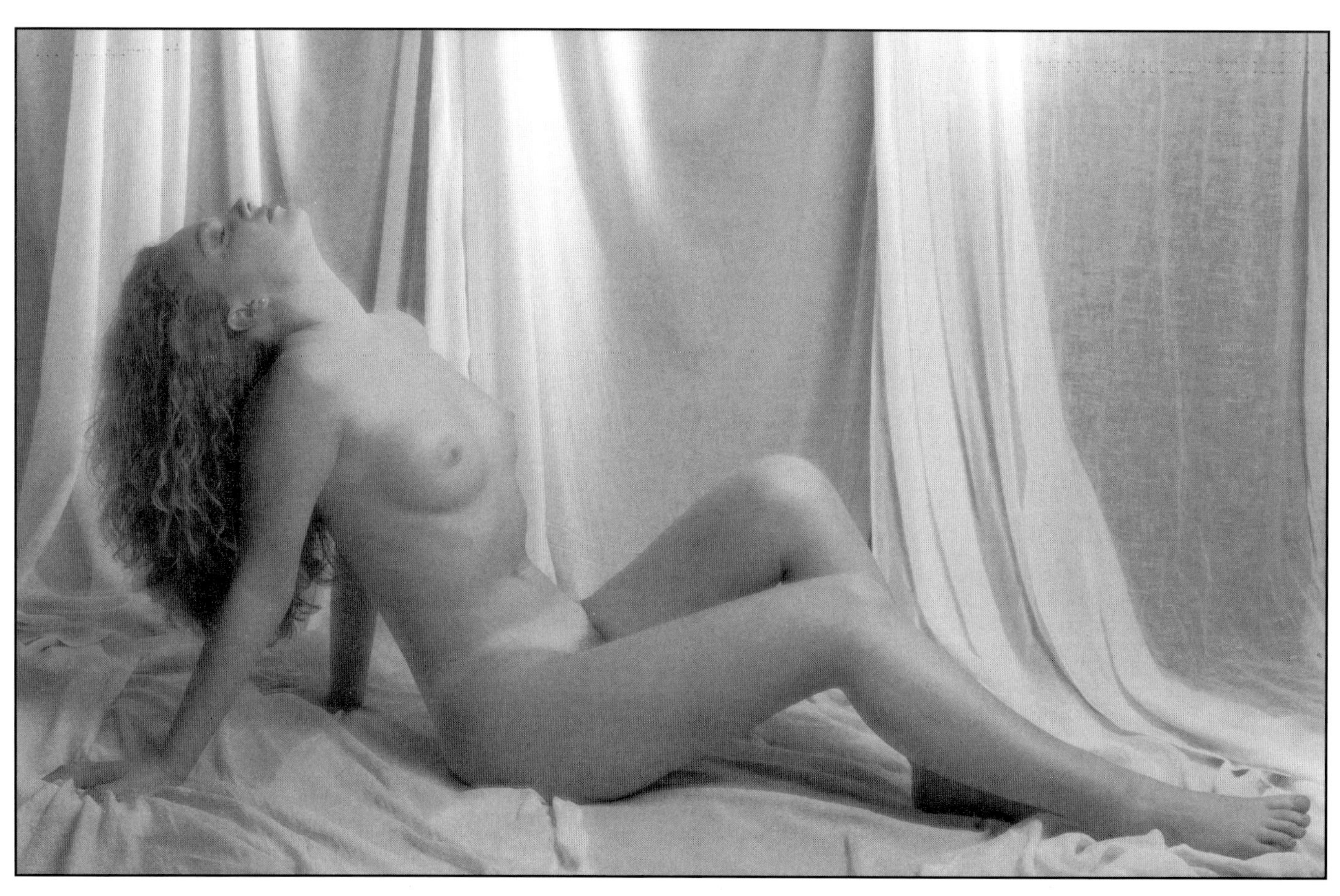

plate 20

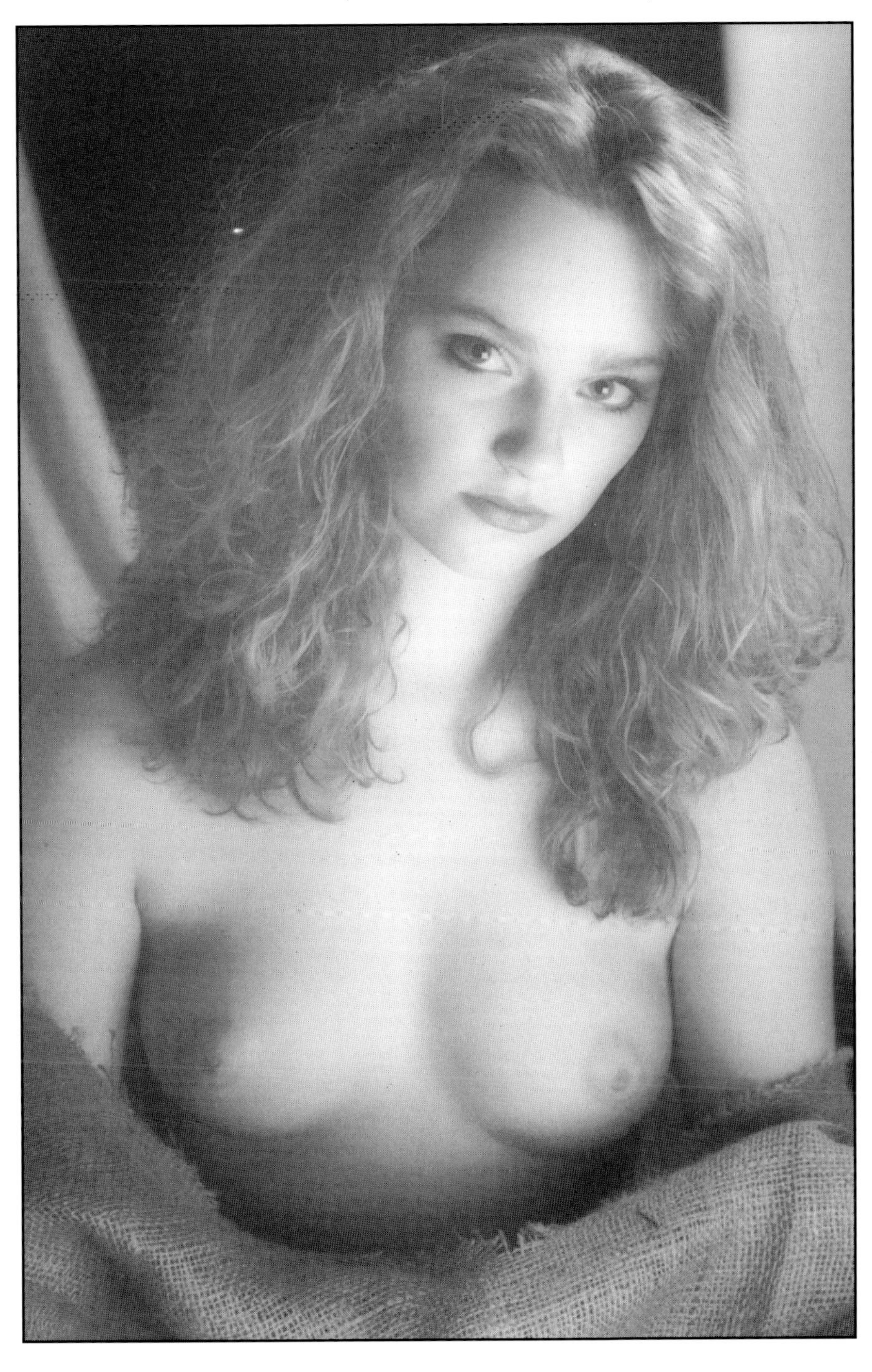

plate 21

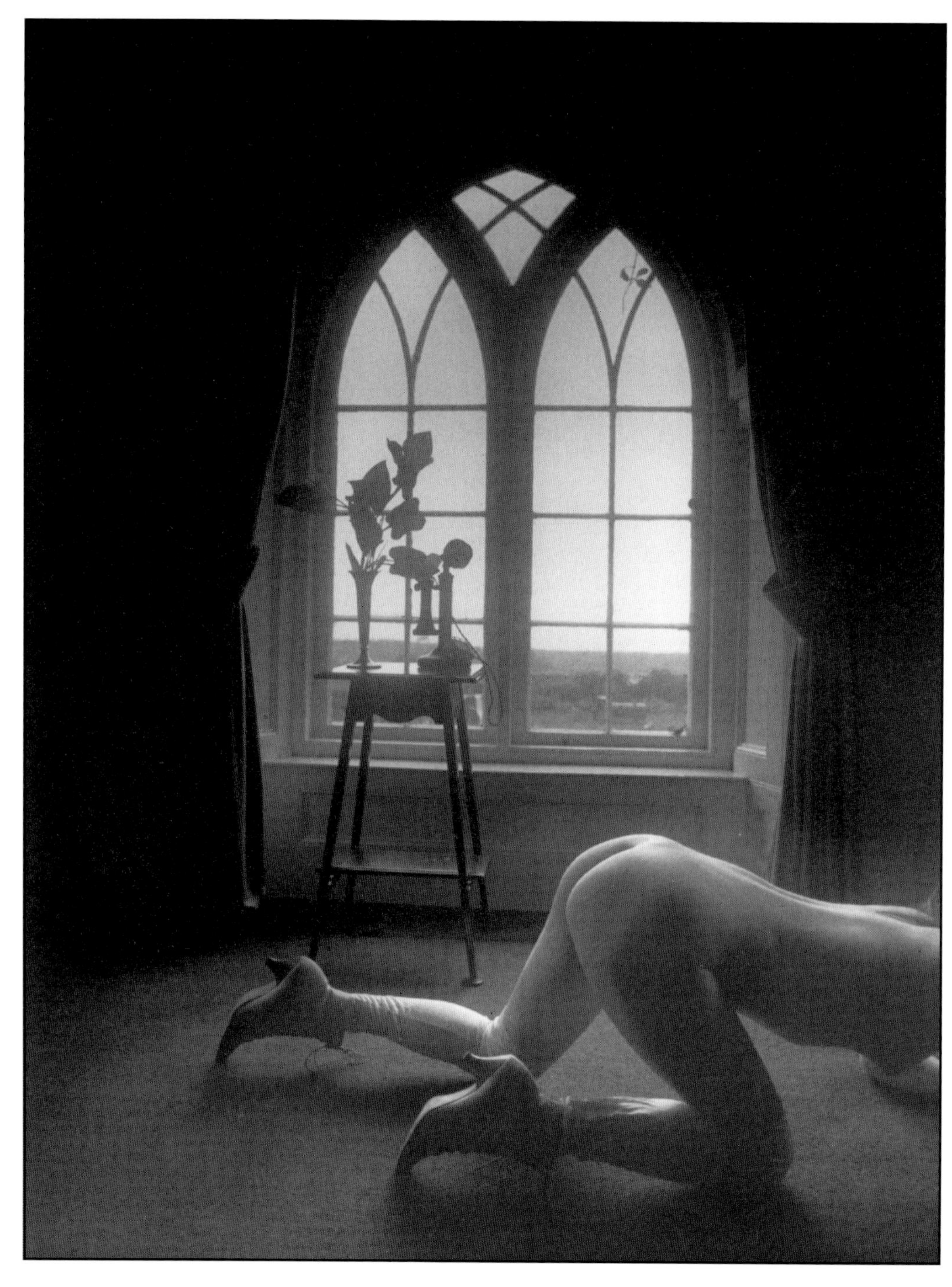

plate 22

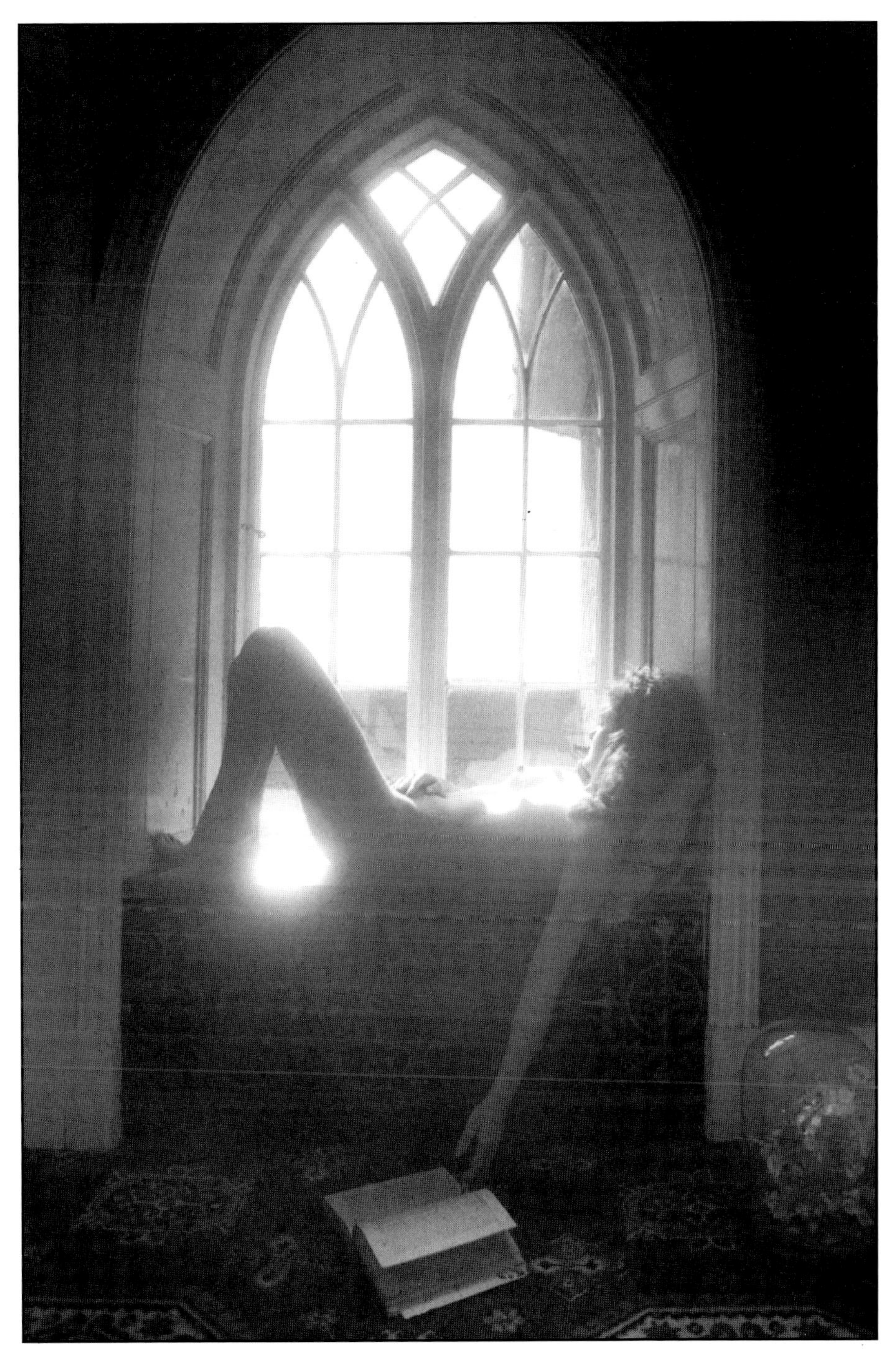

plate 23

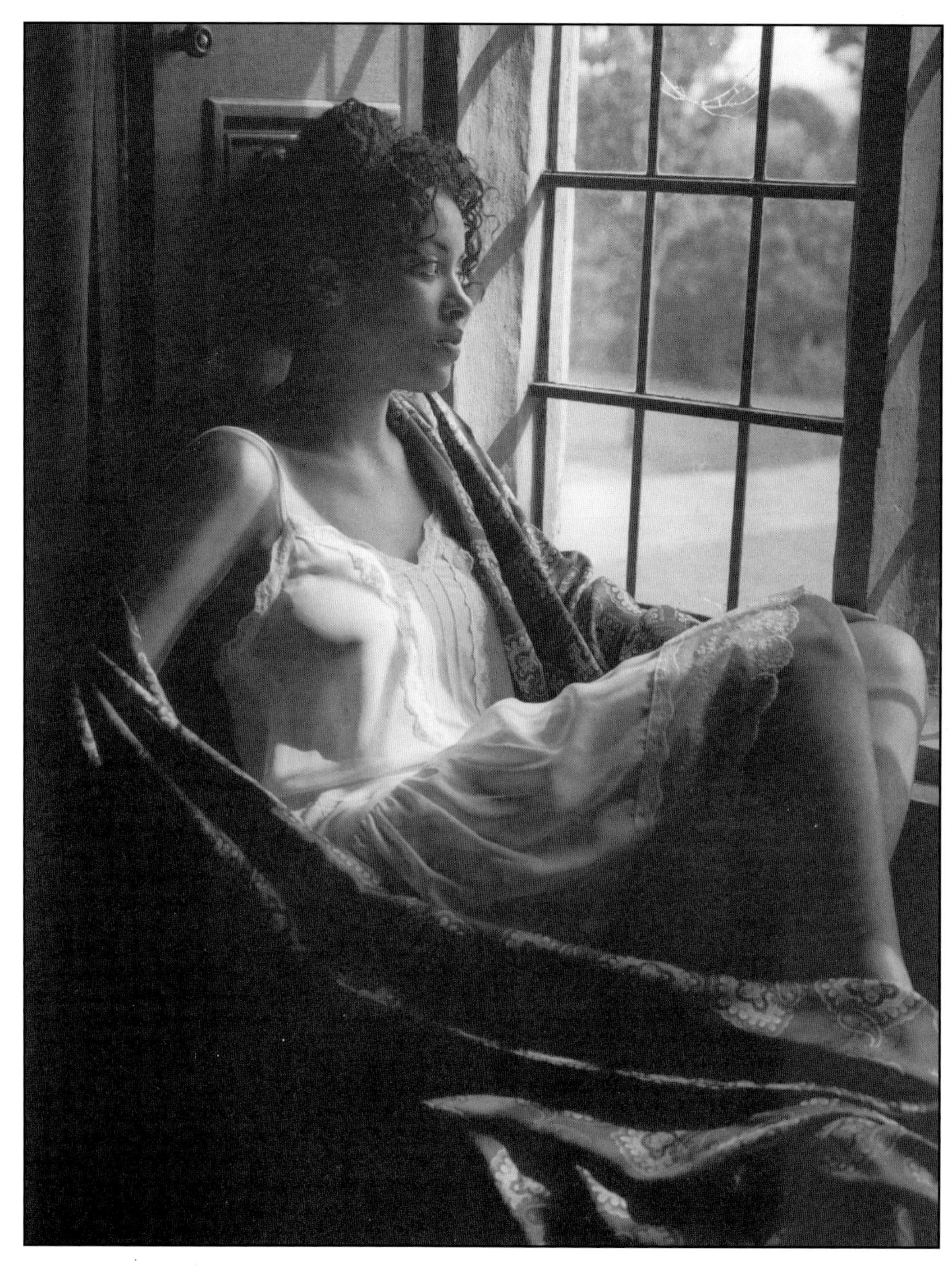

plate 24

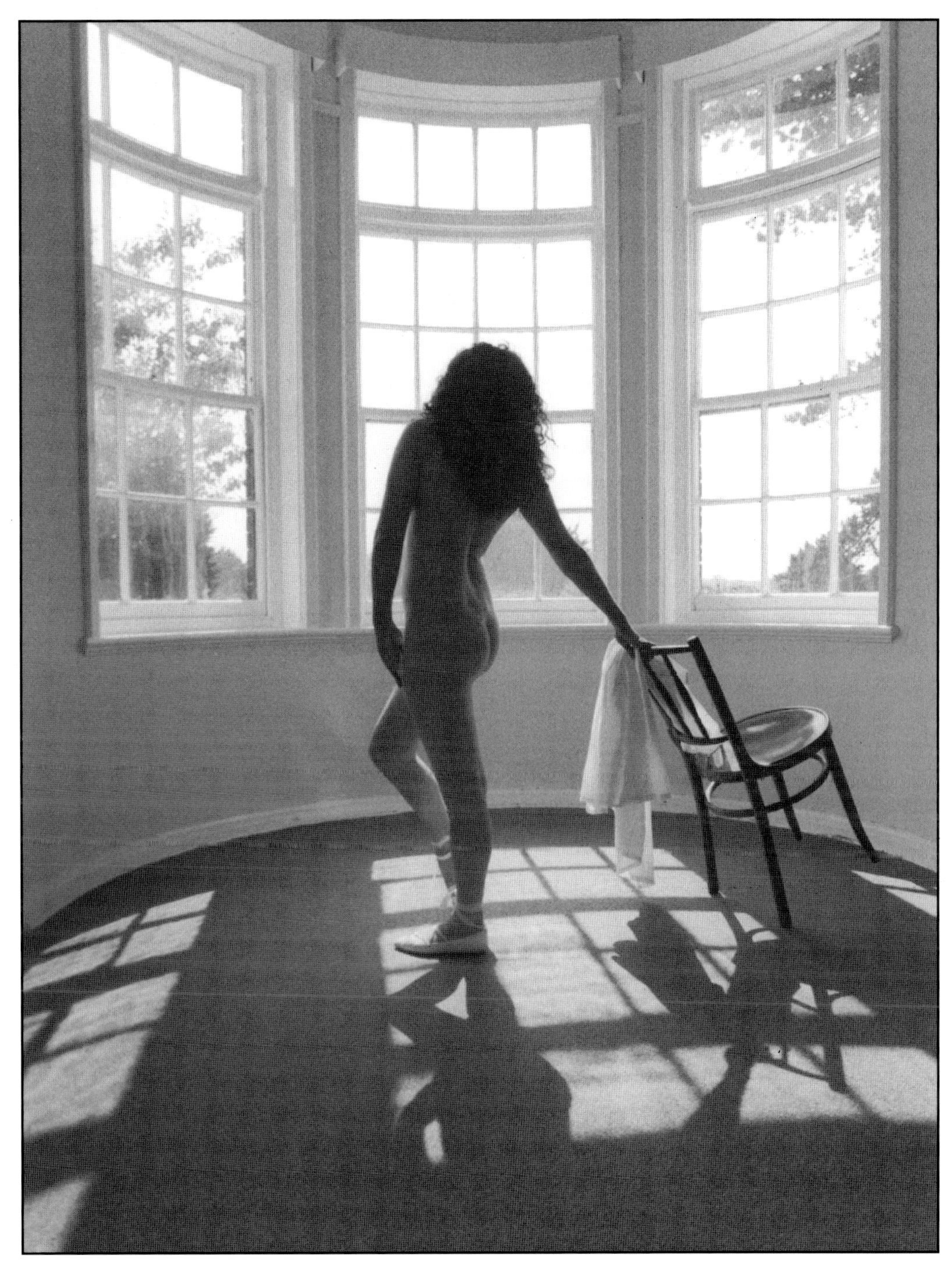

plate 25

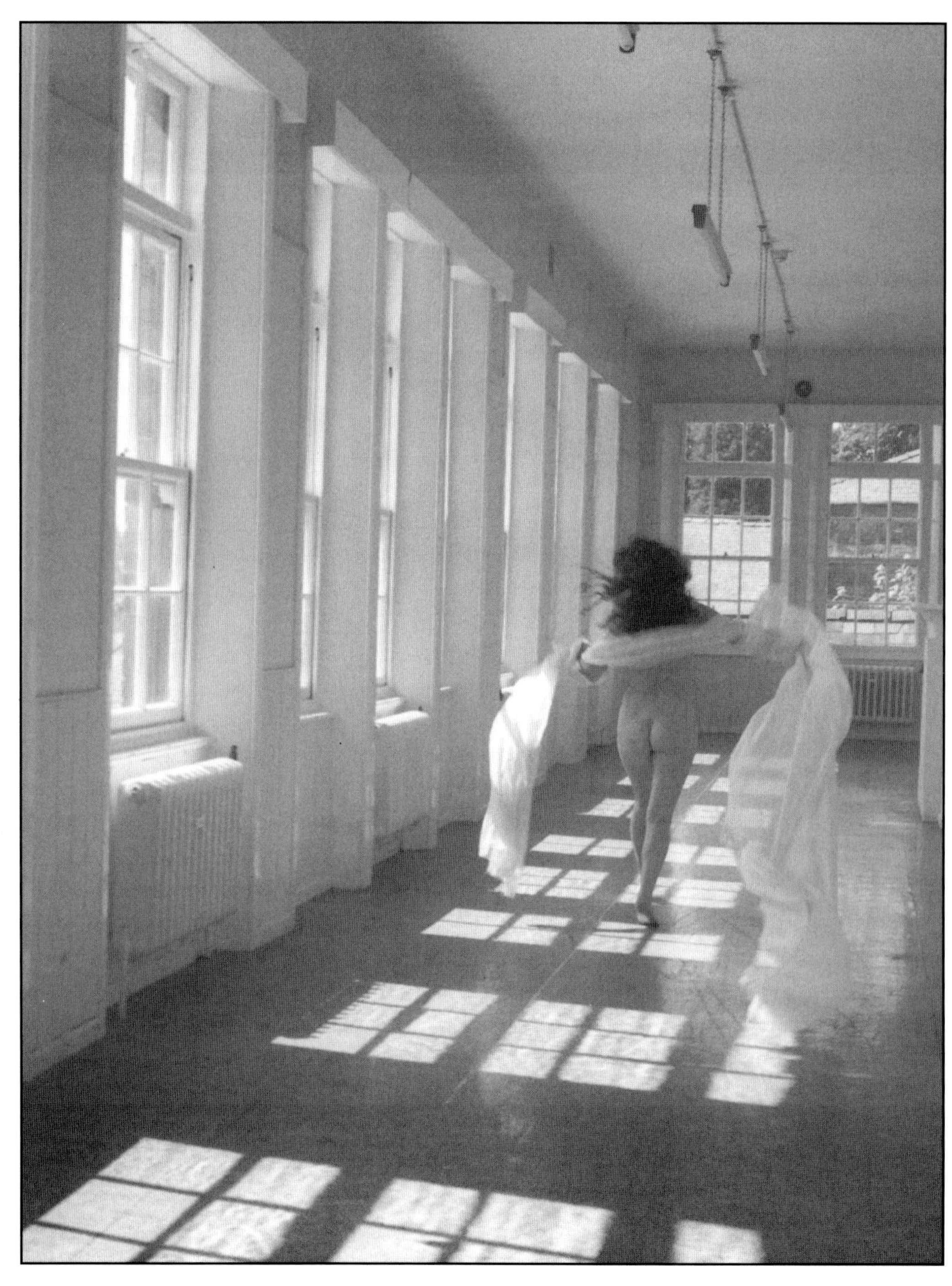

plate 26

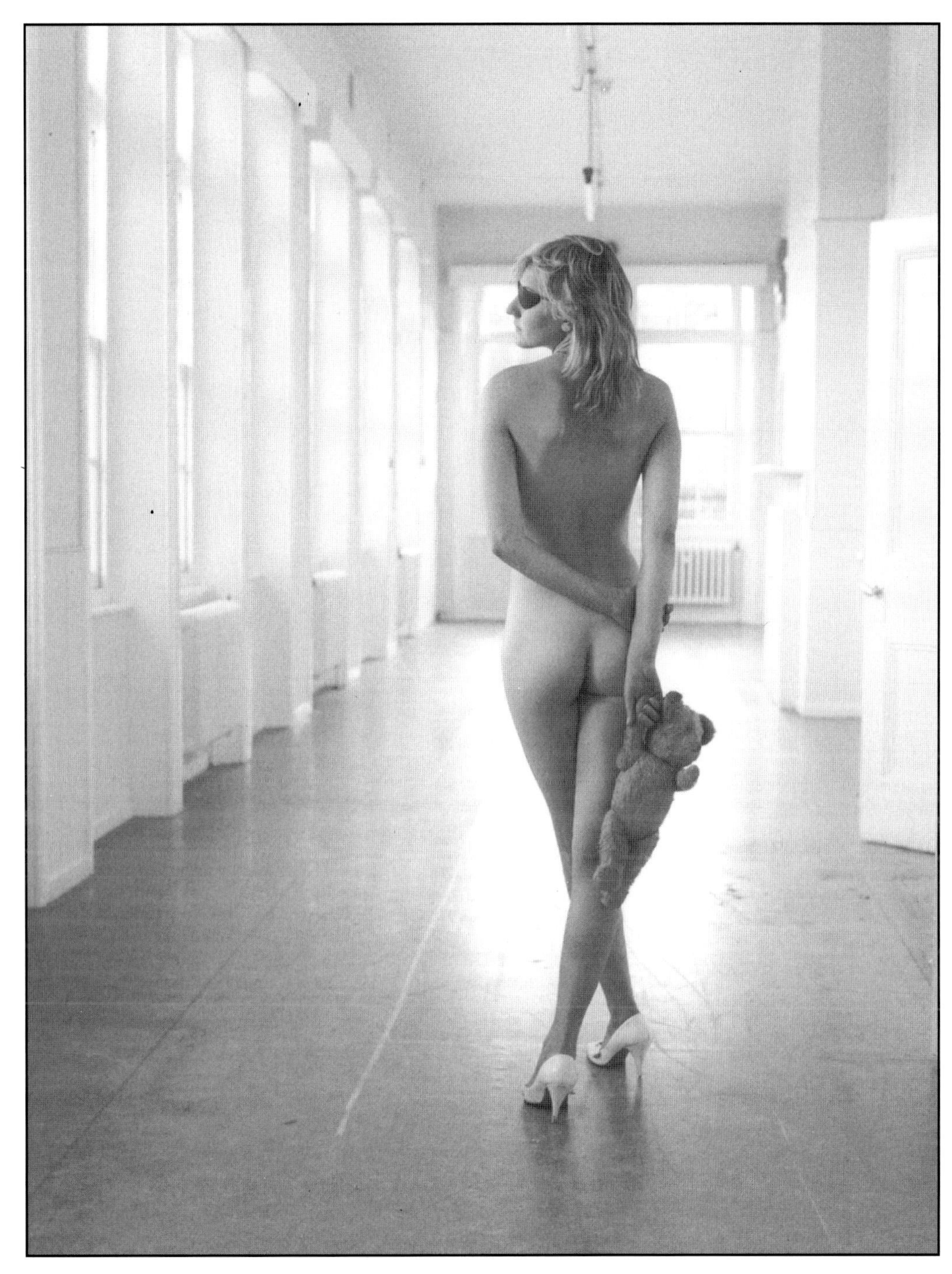

plate 27

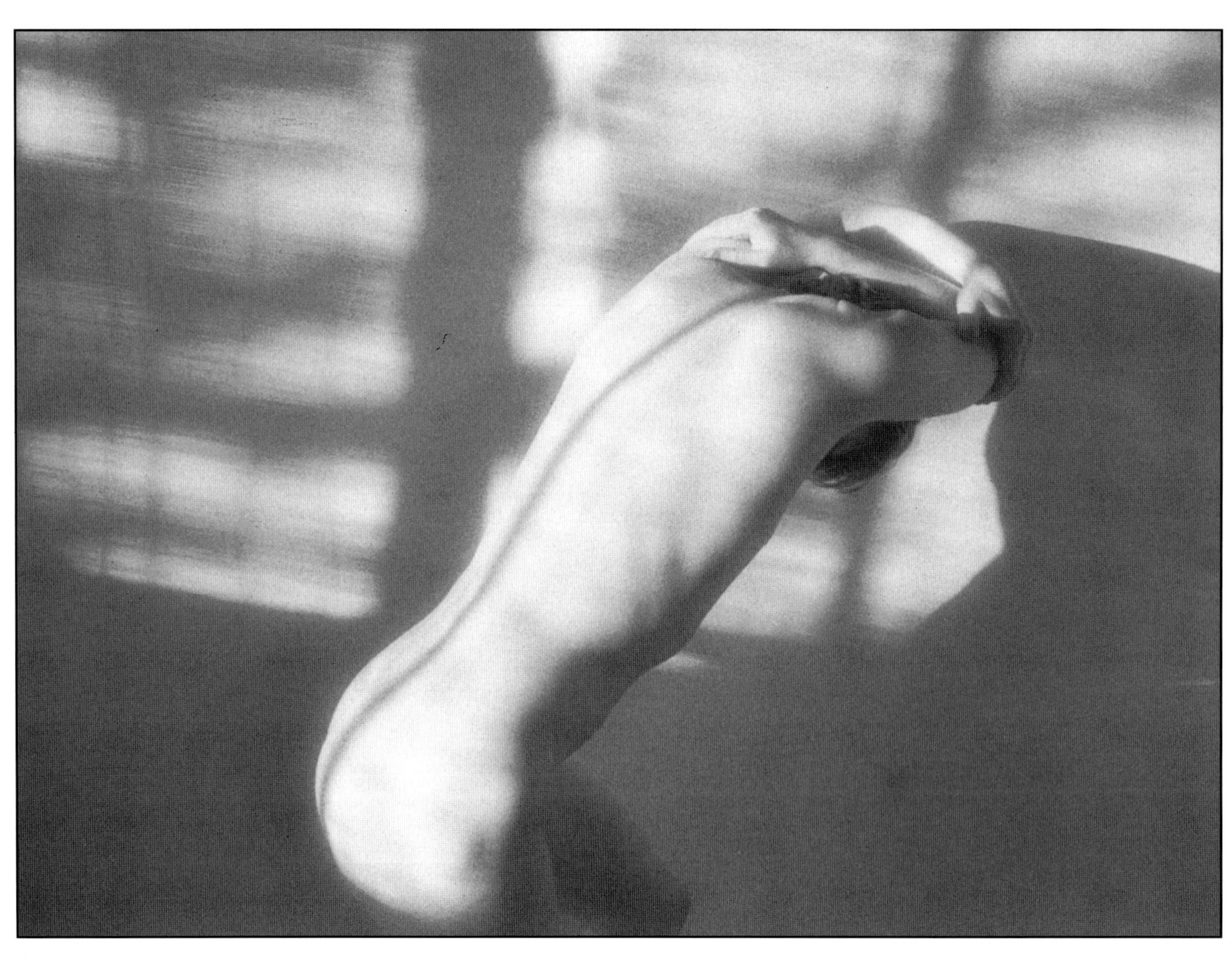

plate 28

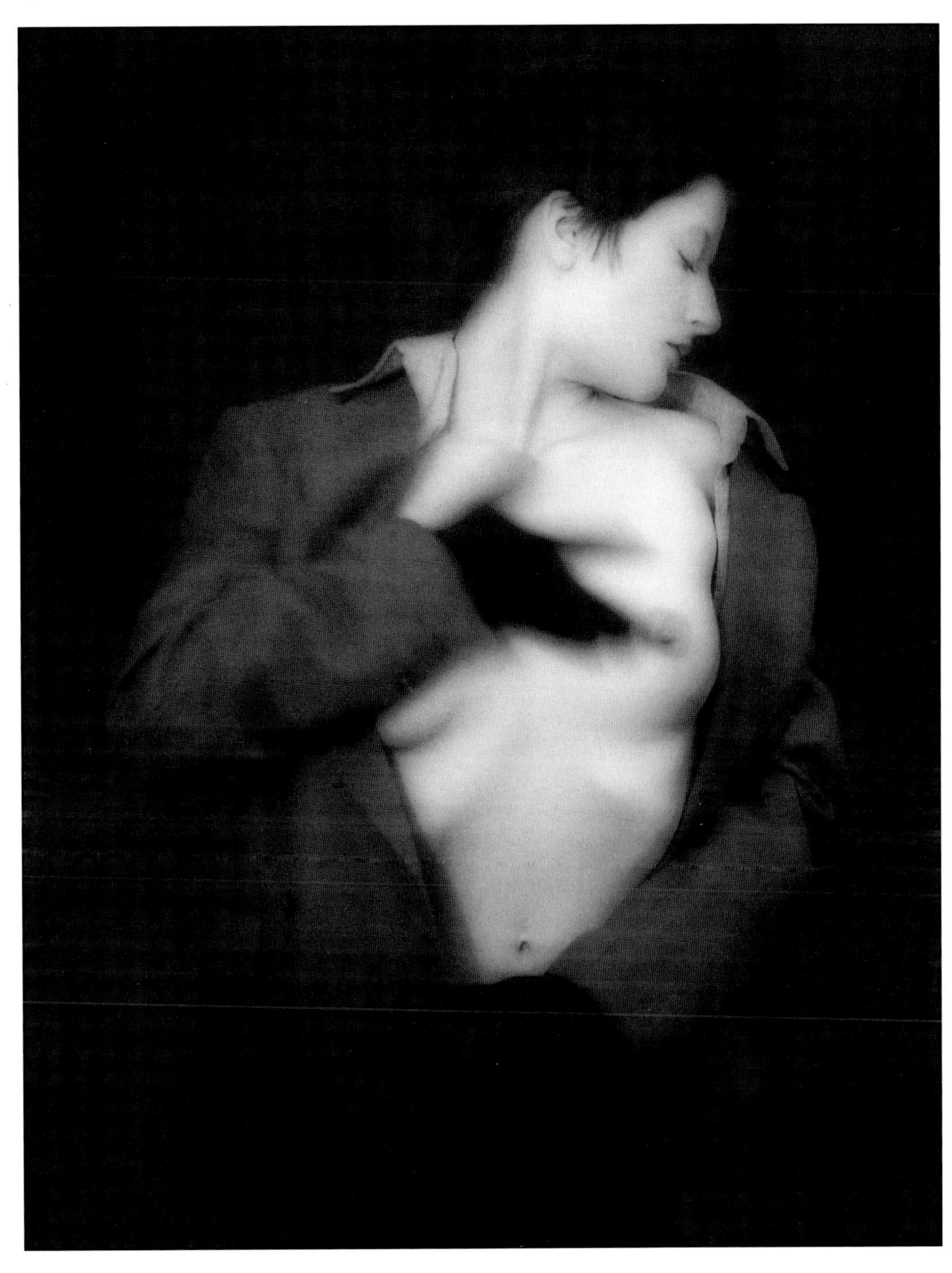

plate 29

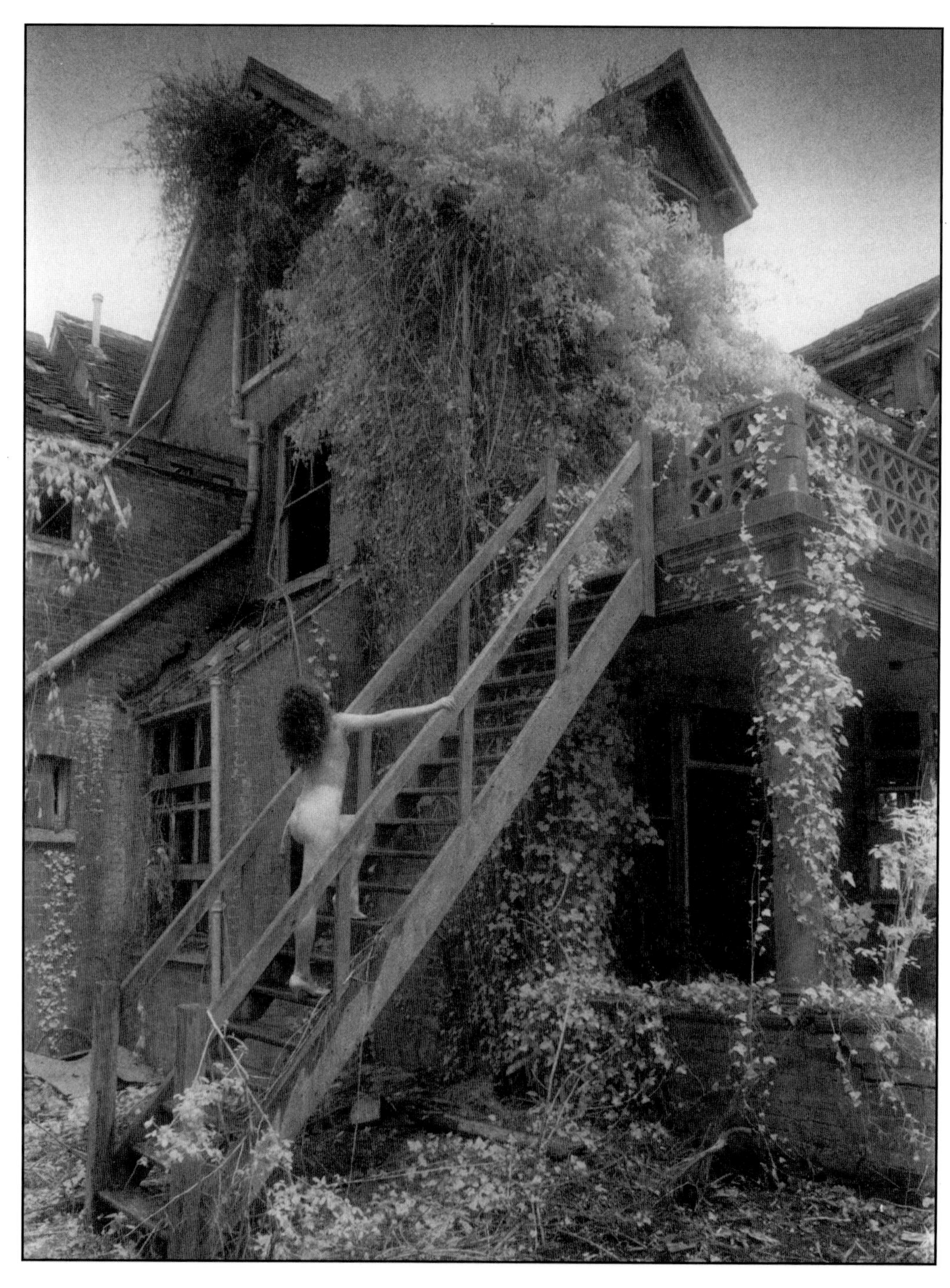

plate 30

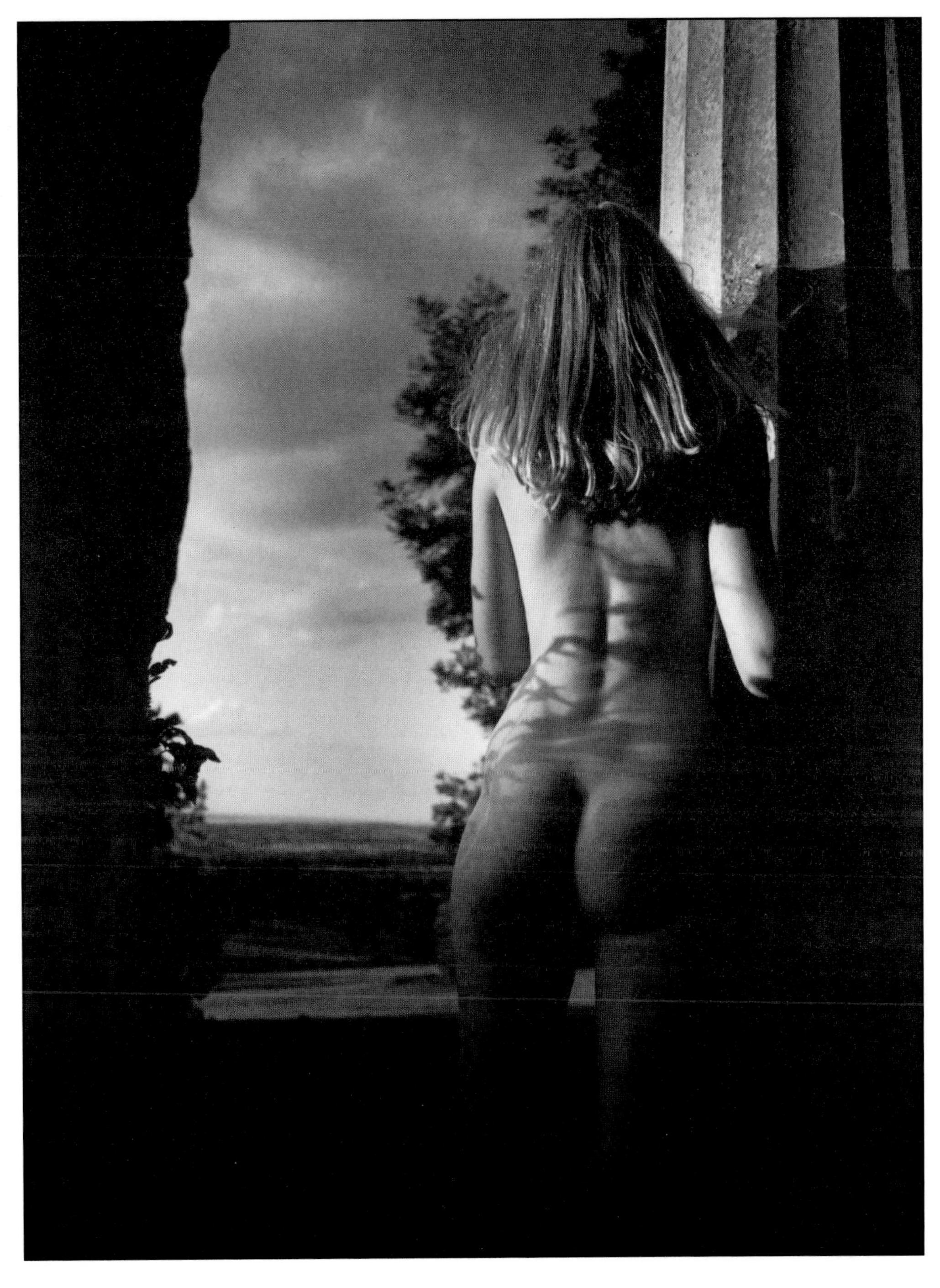

plate 31

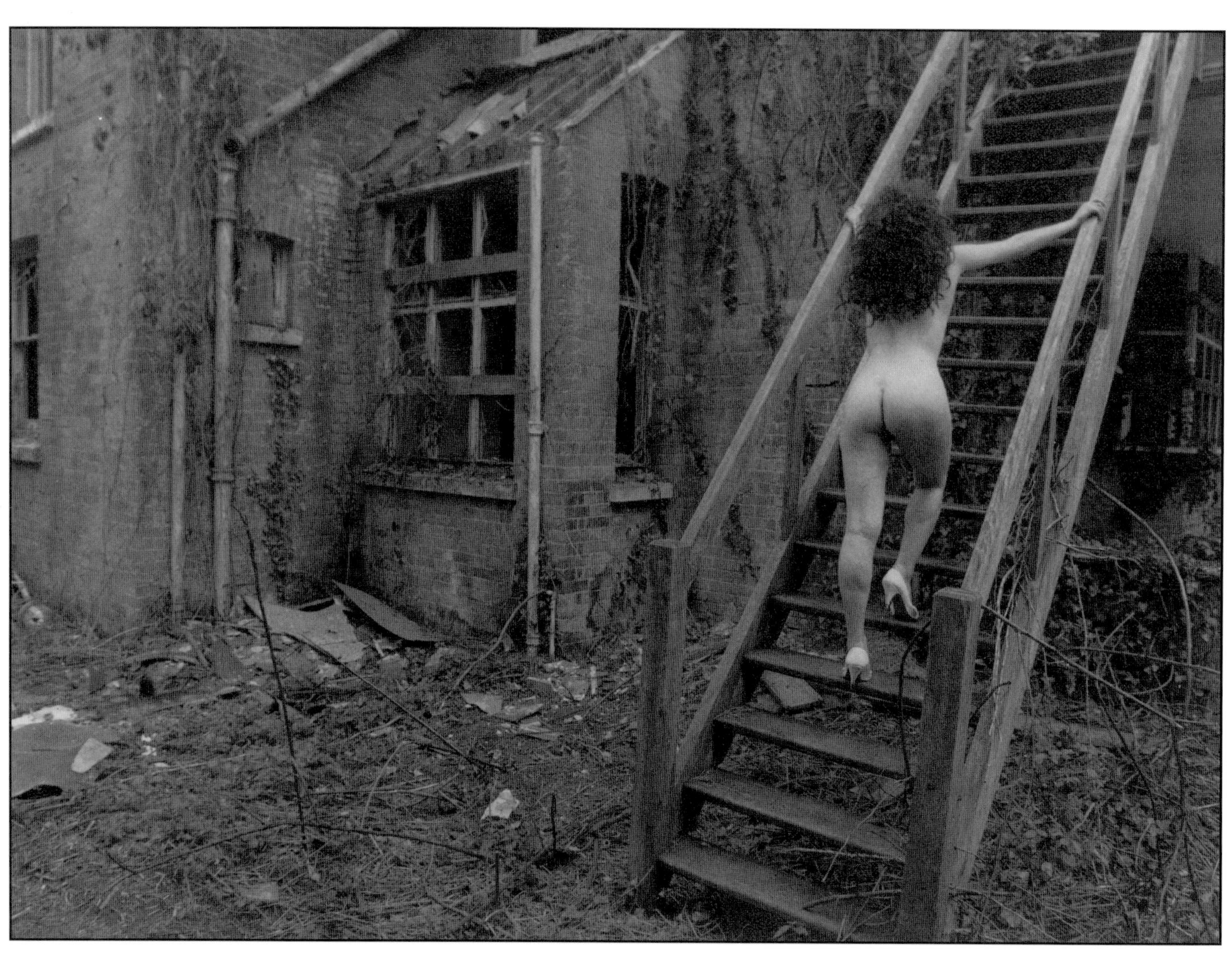

plate 32

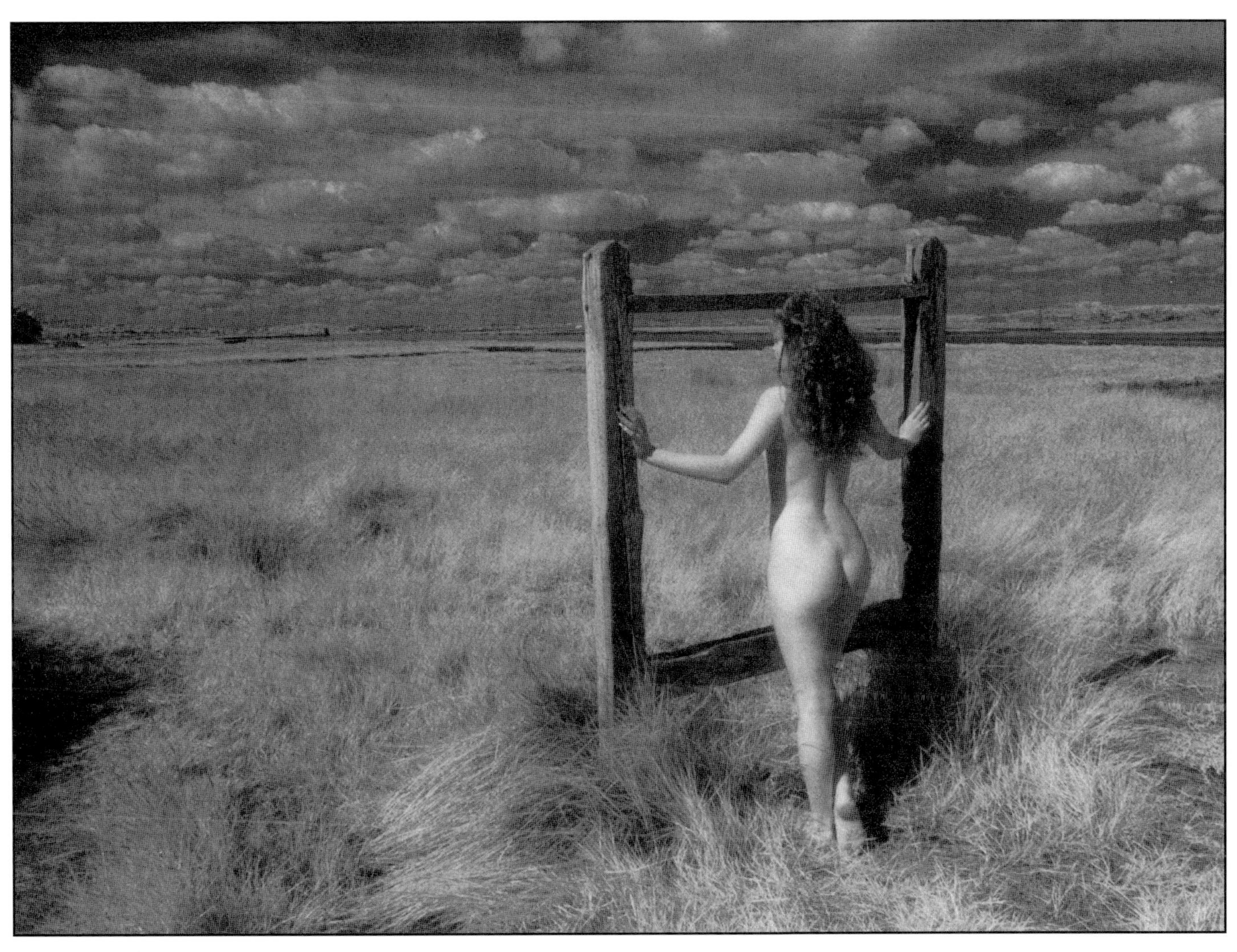

plate 33

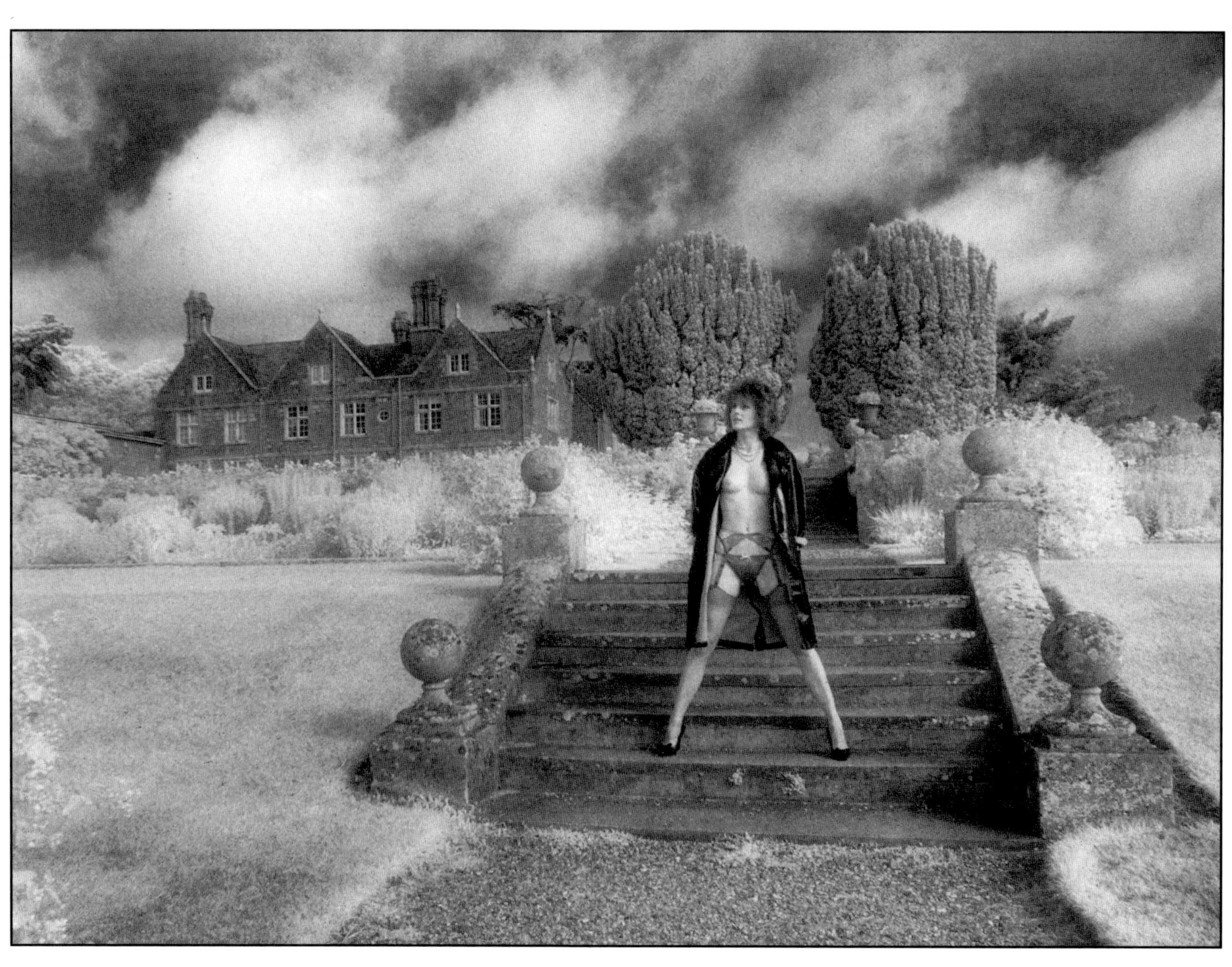

plate 34

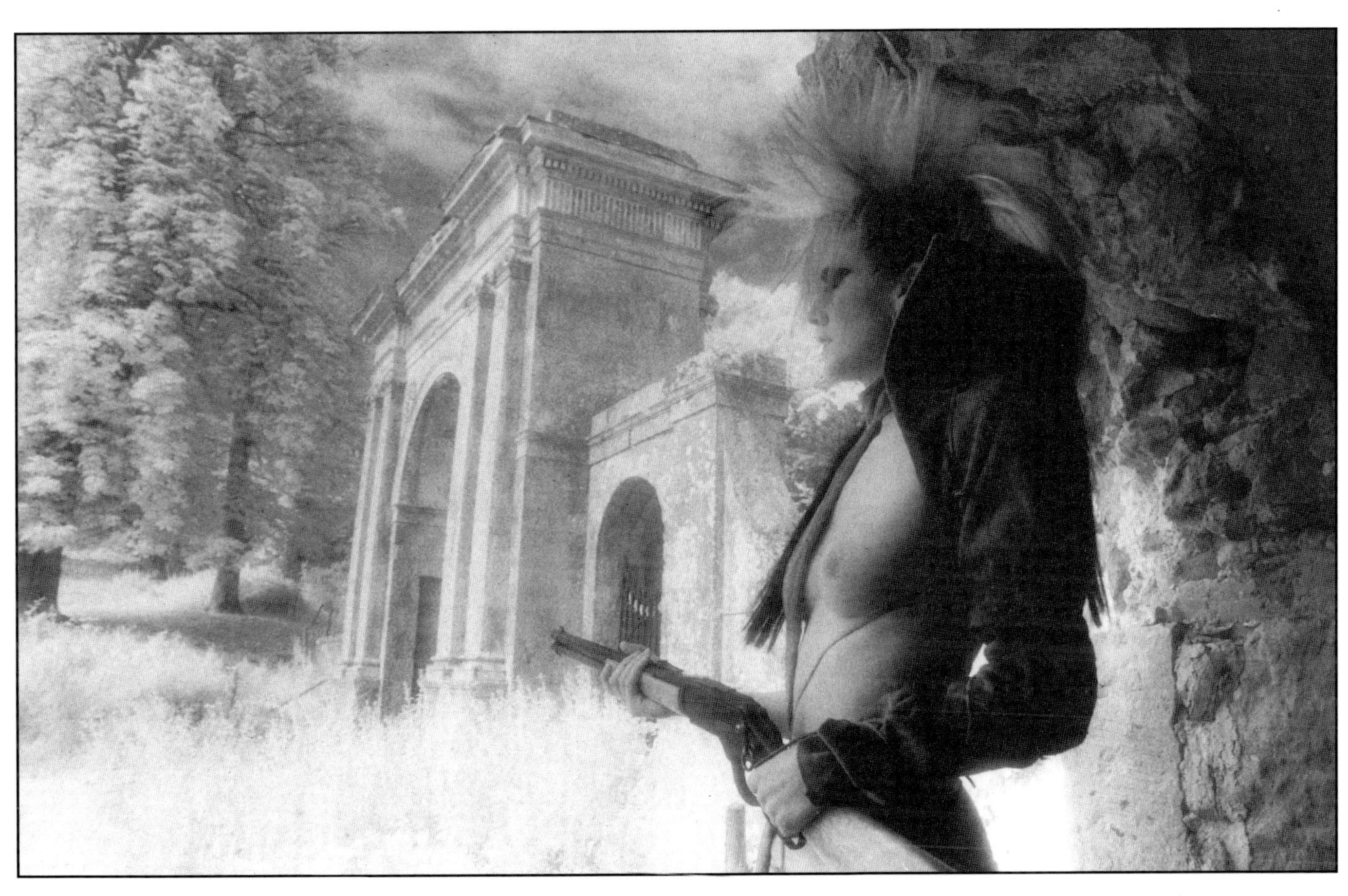

plate 3 5

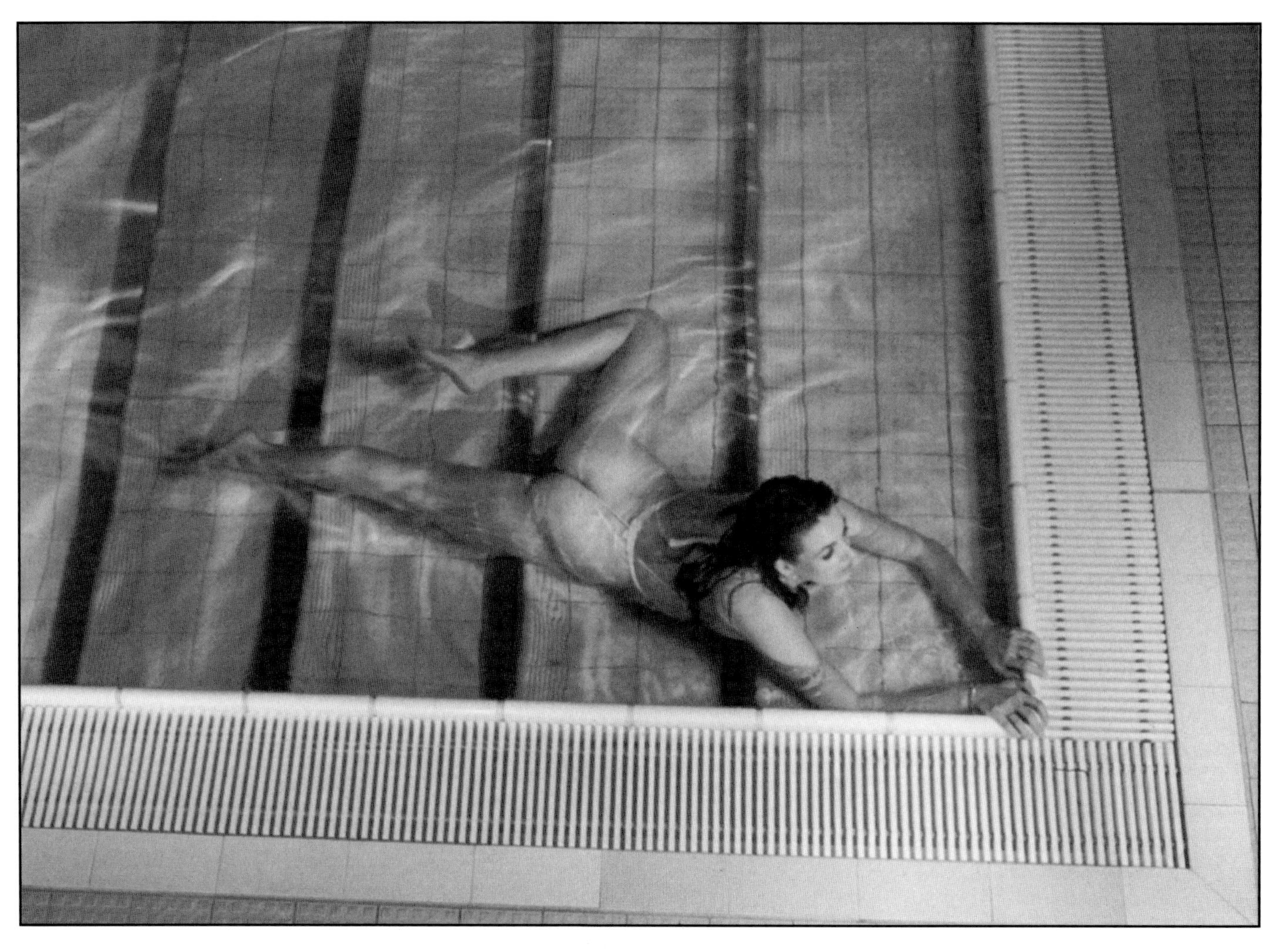

plate 36

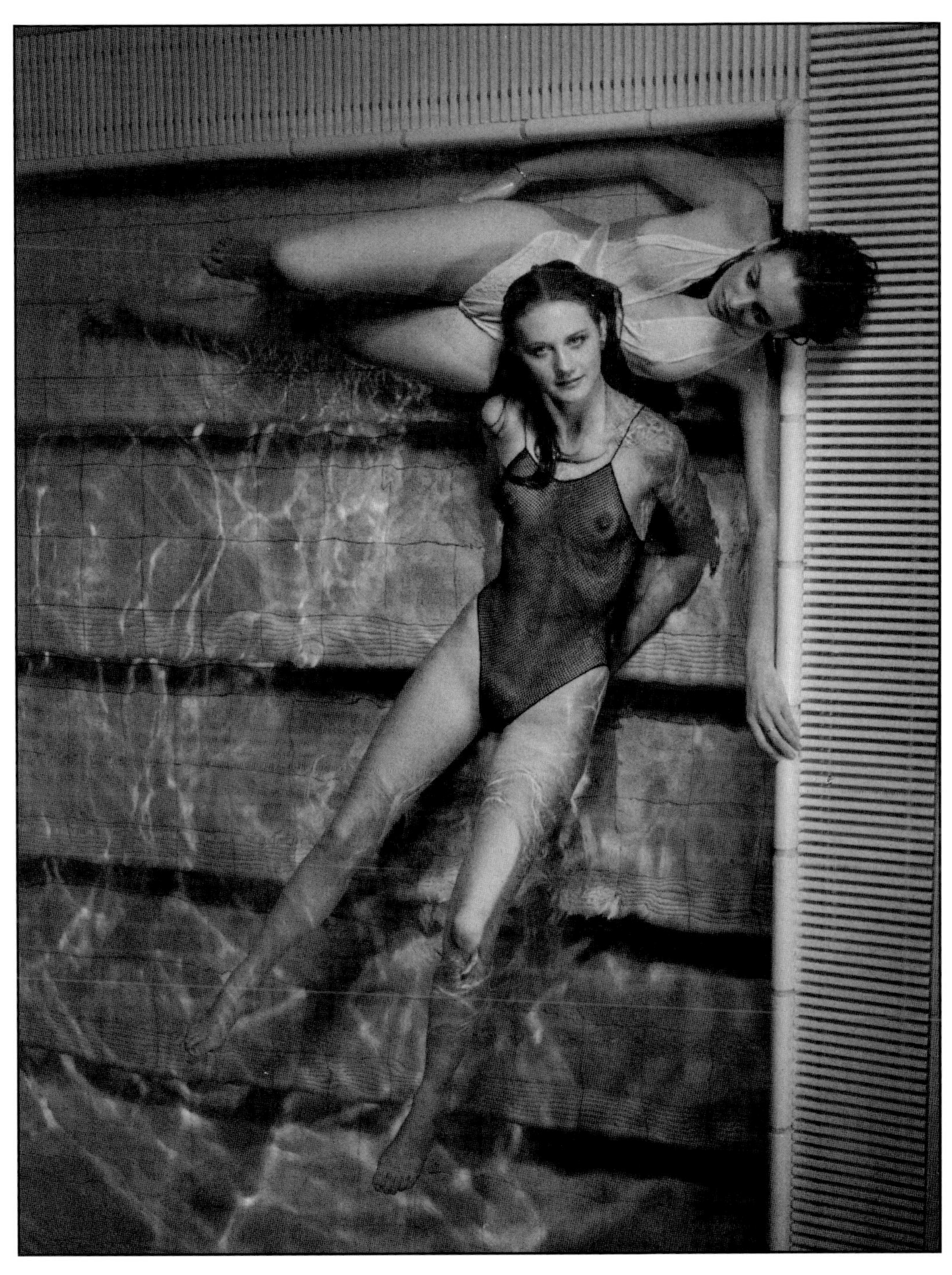

plate 37

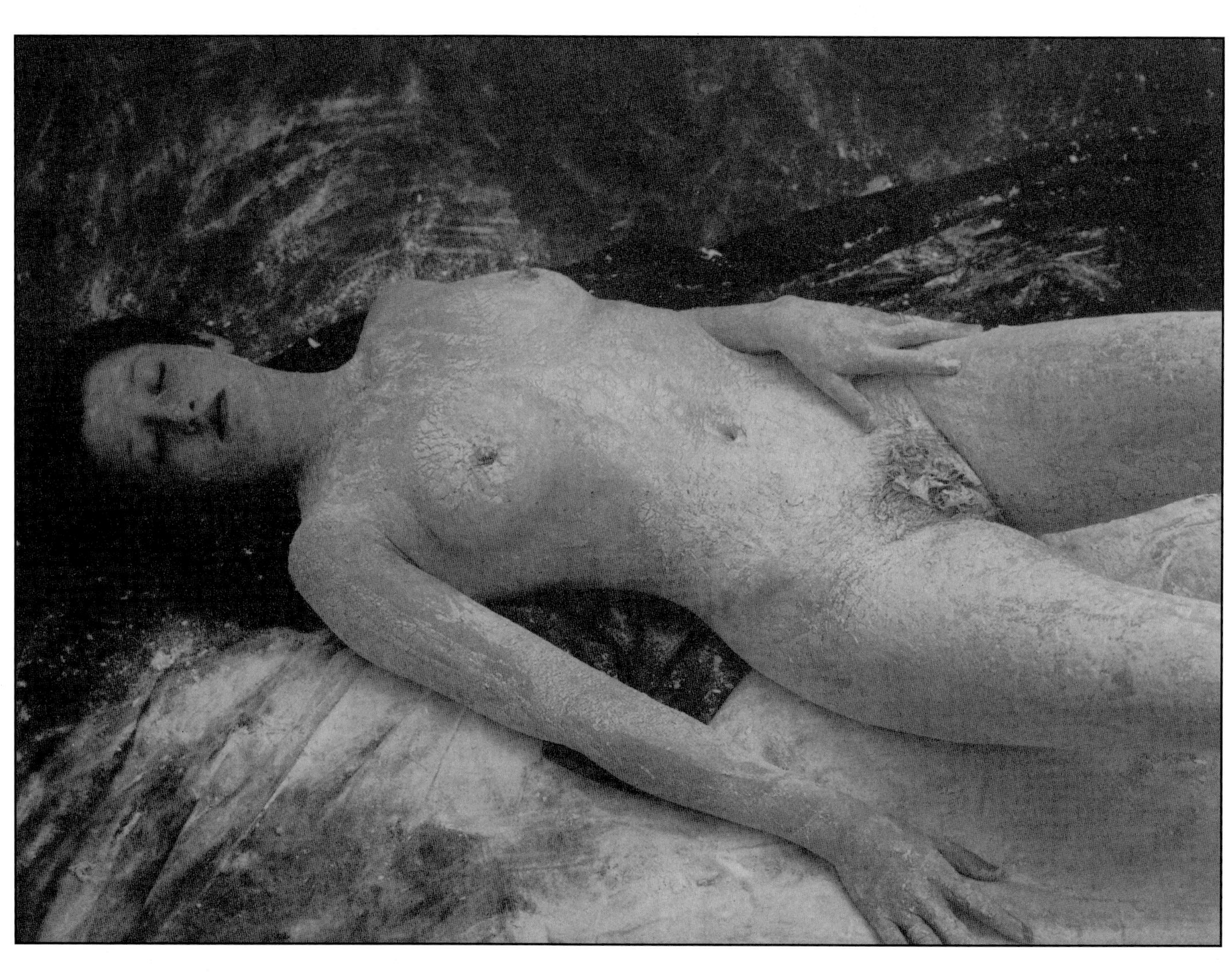

plate 38

42

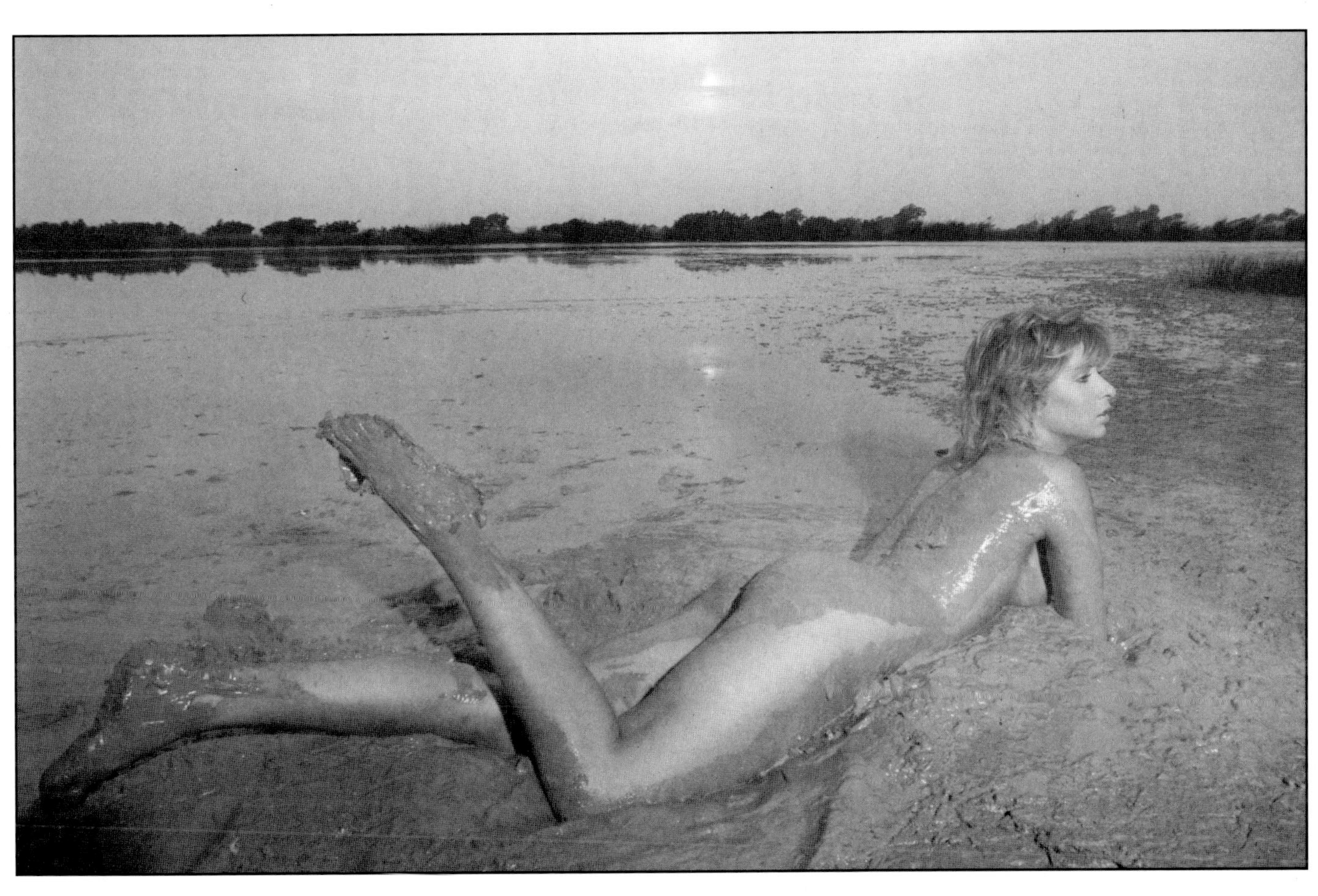

plate 39

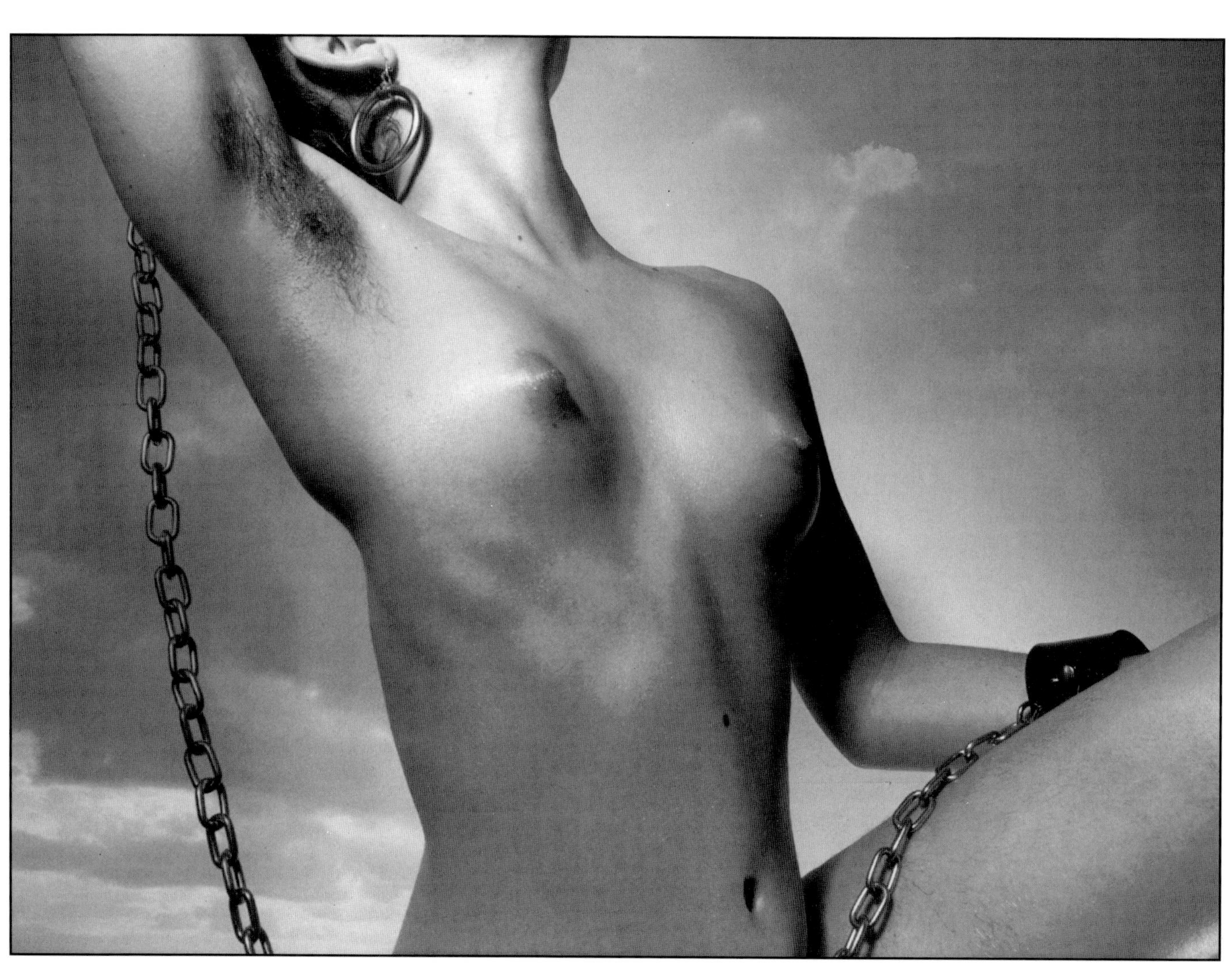

plate 40

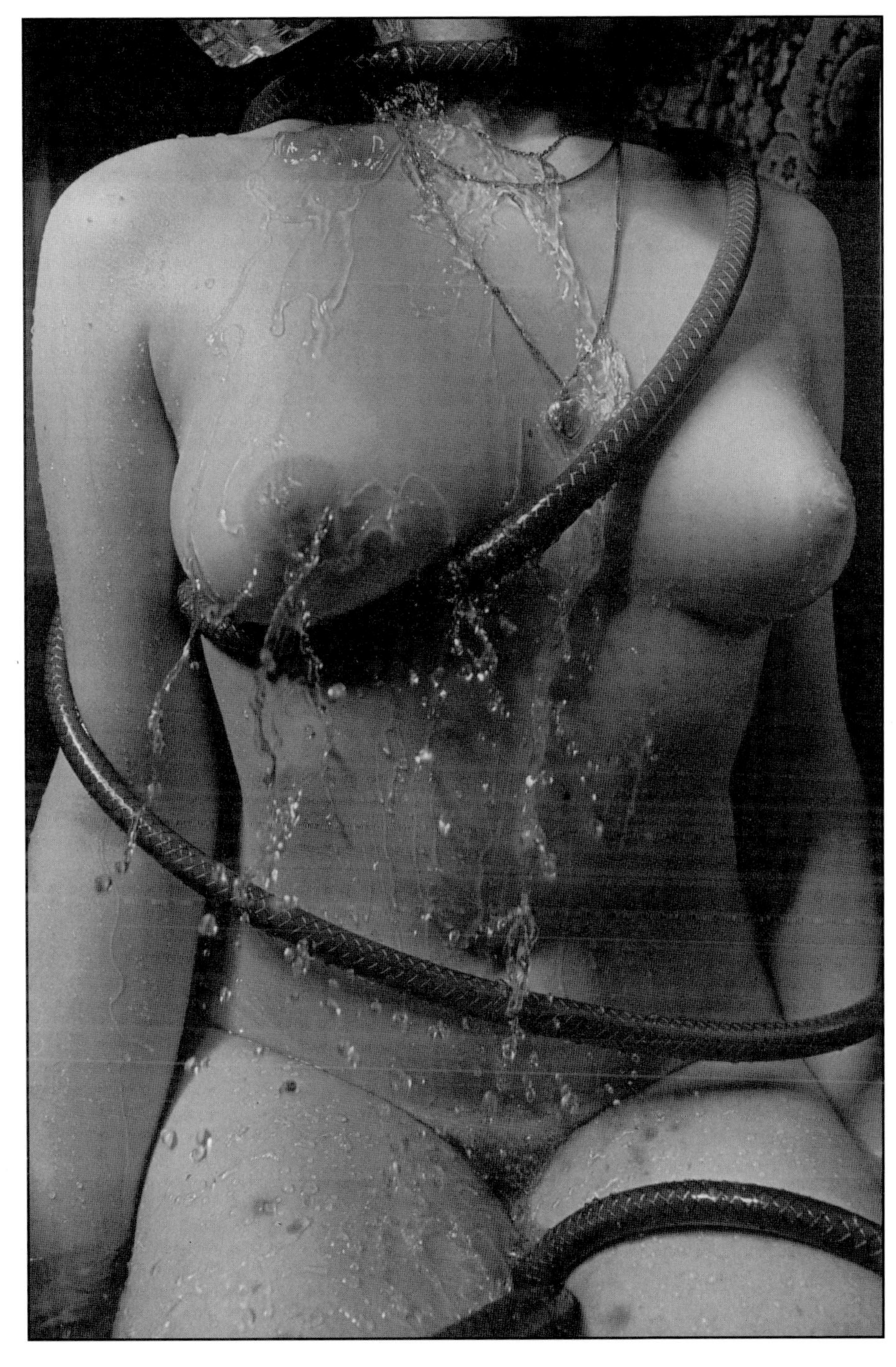

plate 41

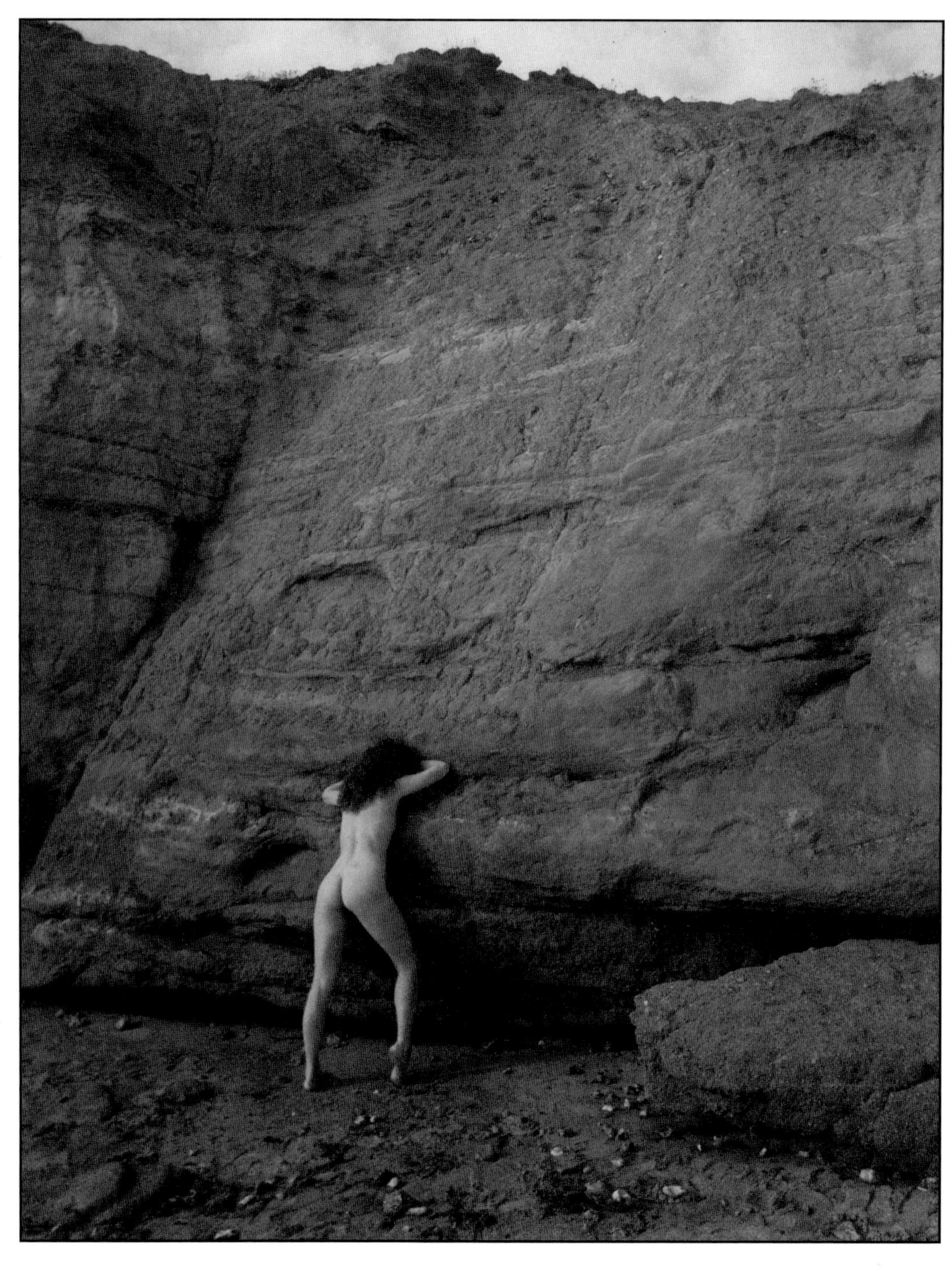

plate 42

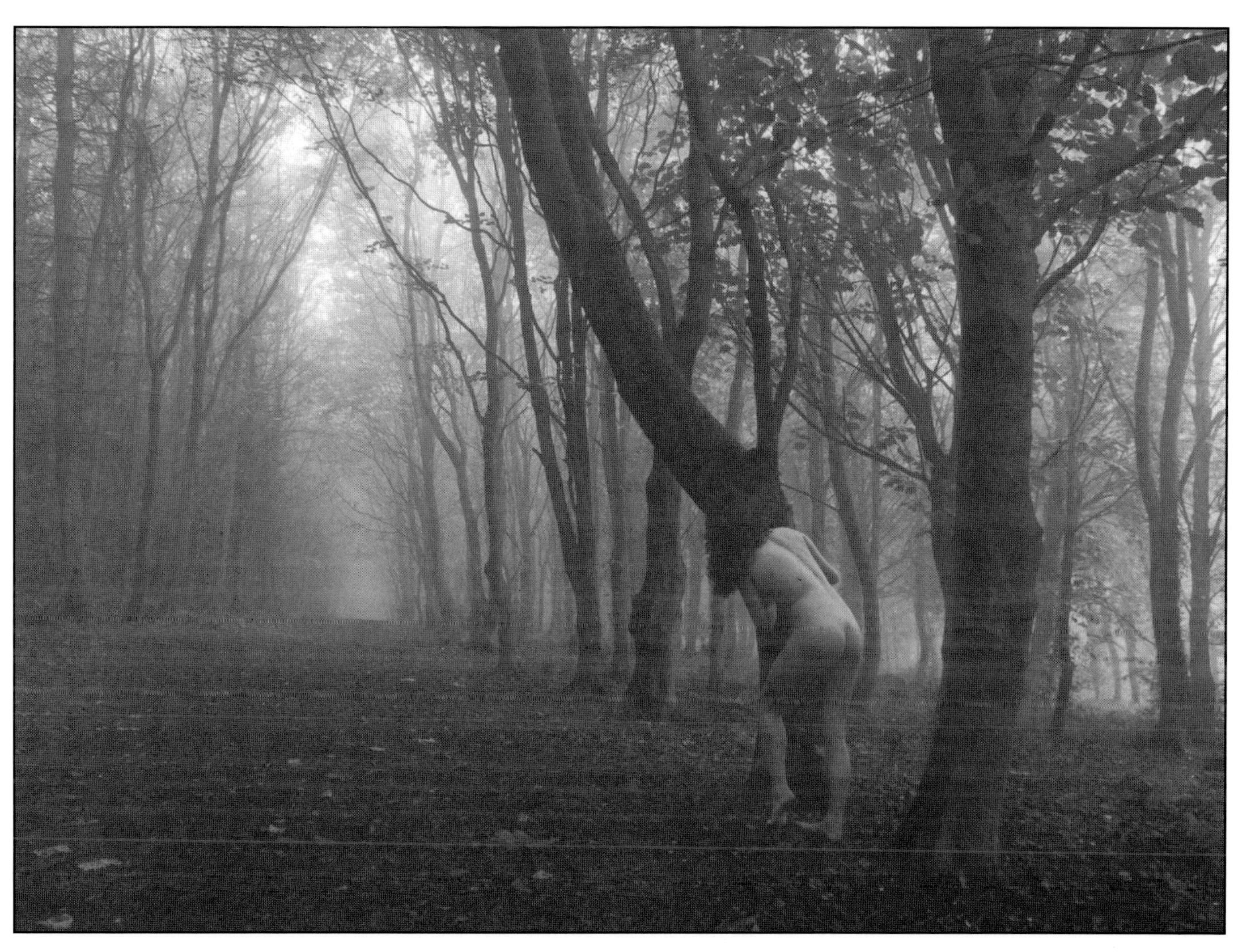

plate 43

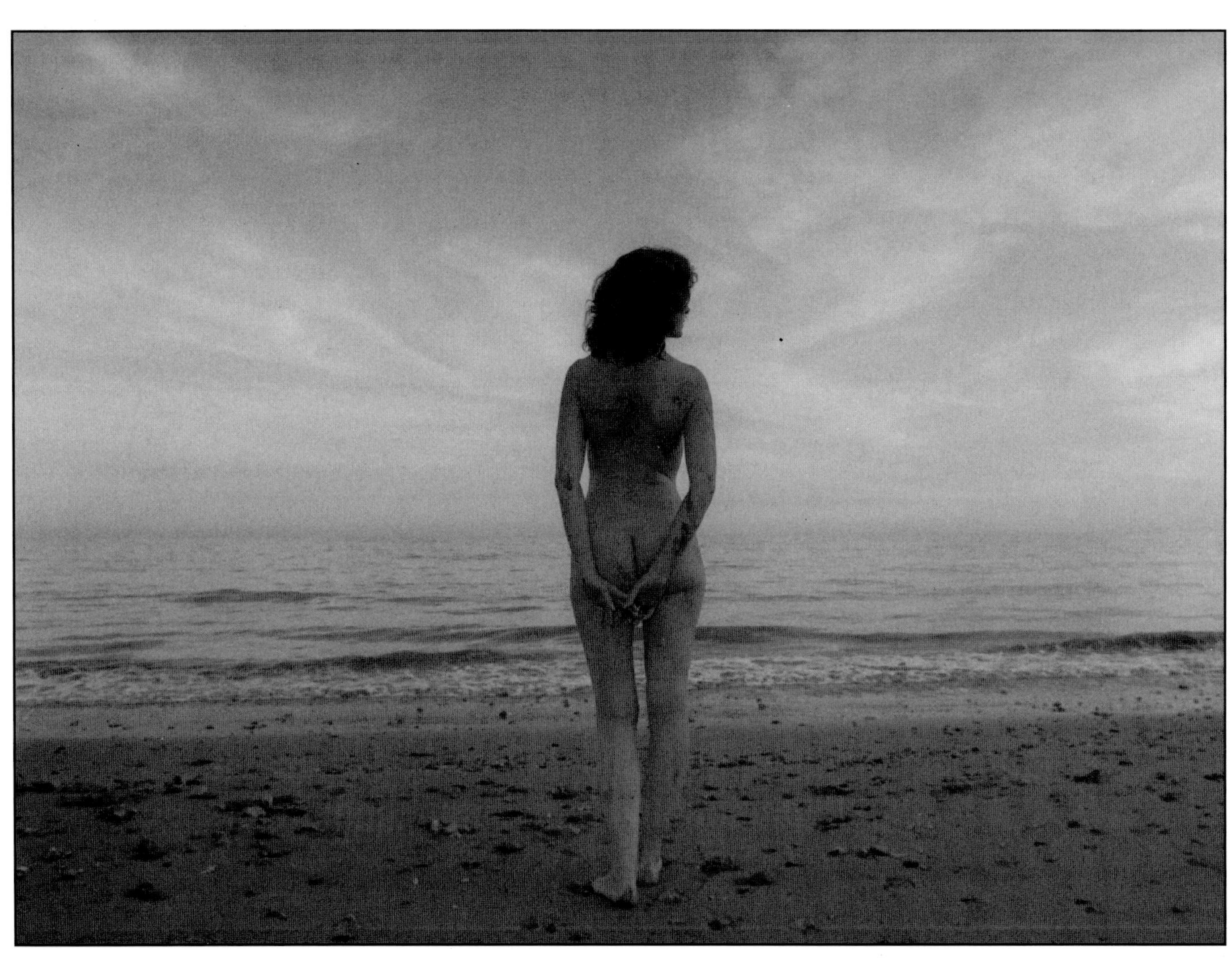

plate 44

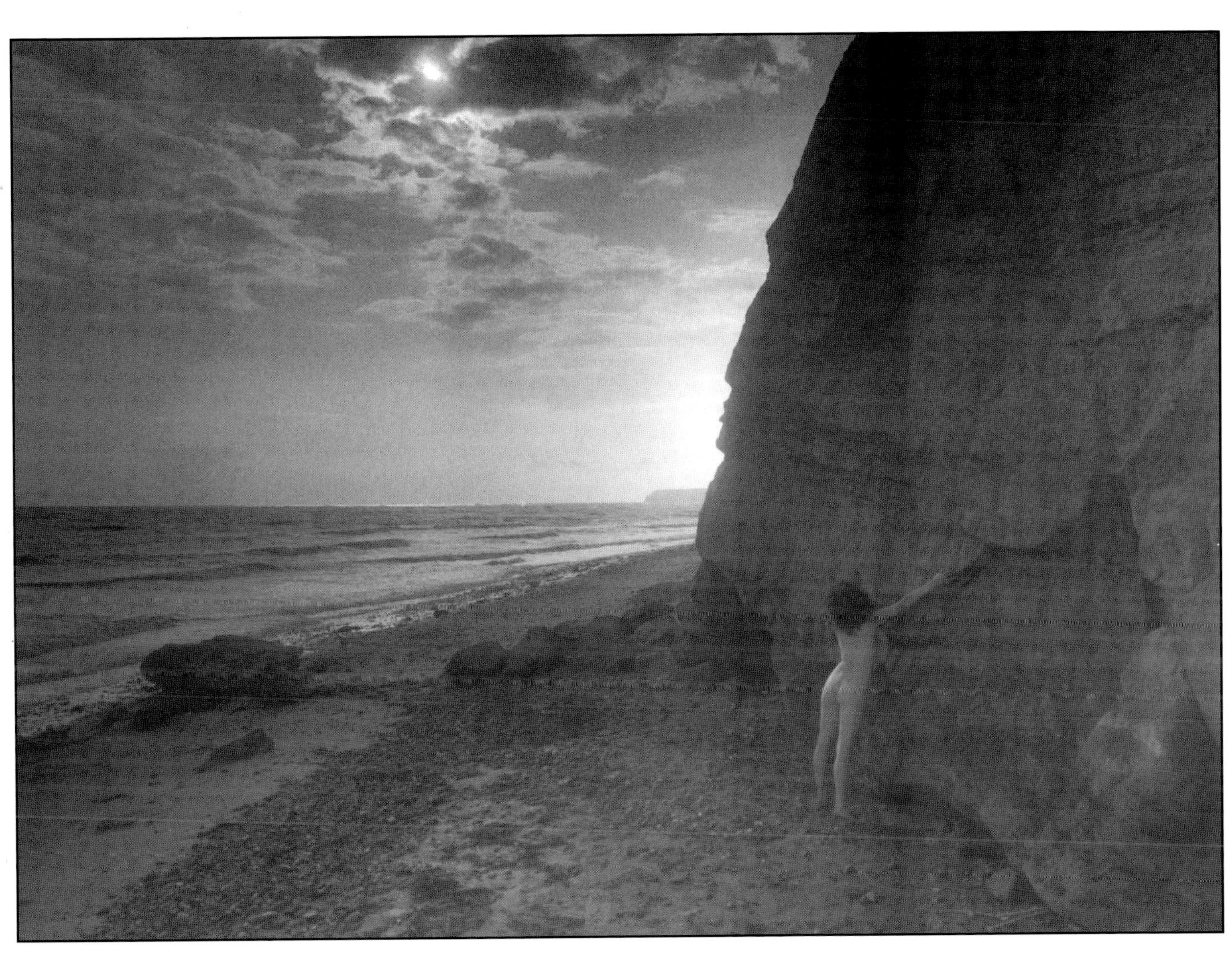

plate 45

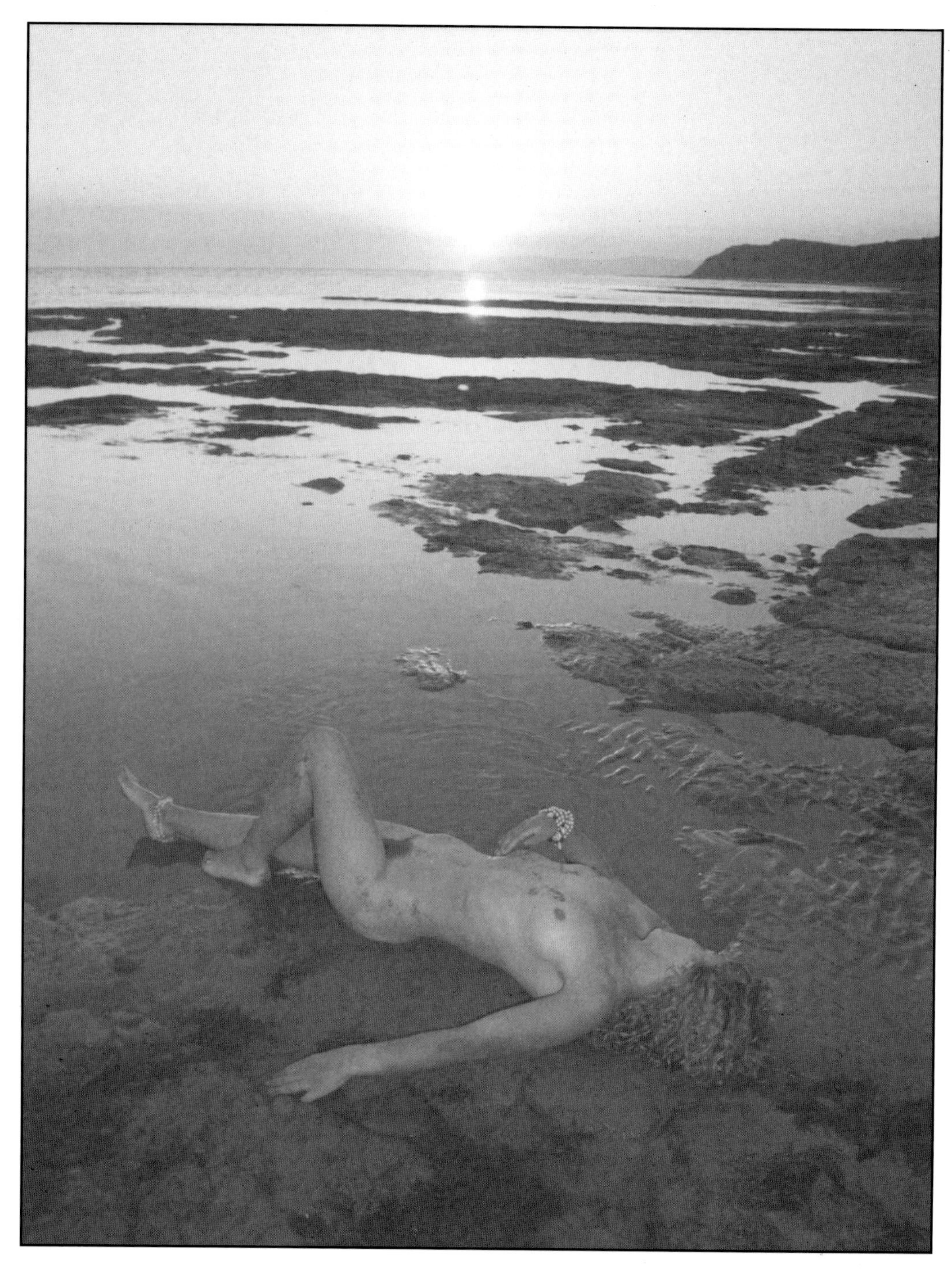

plate 46

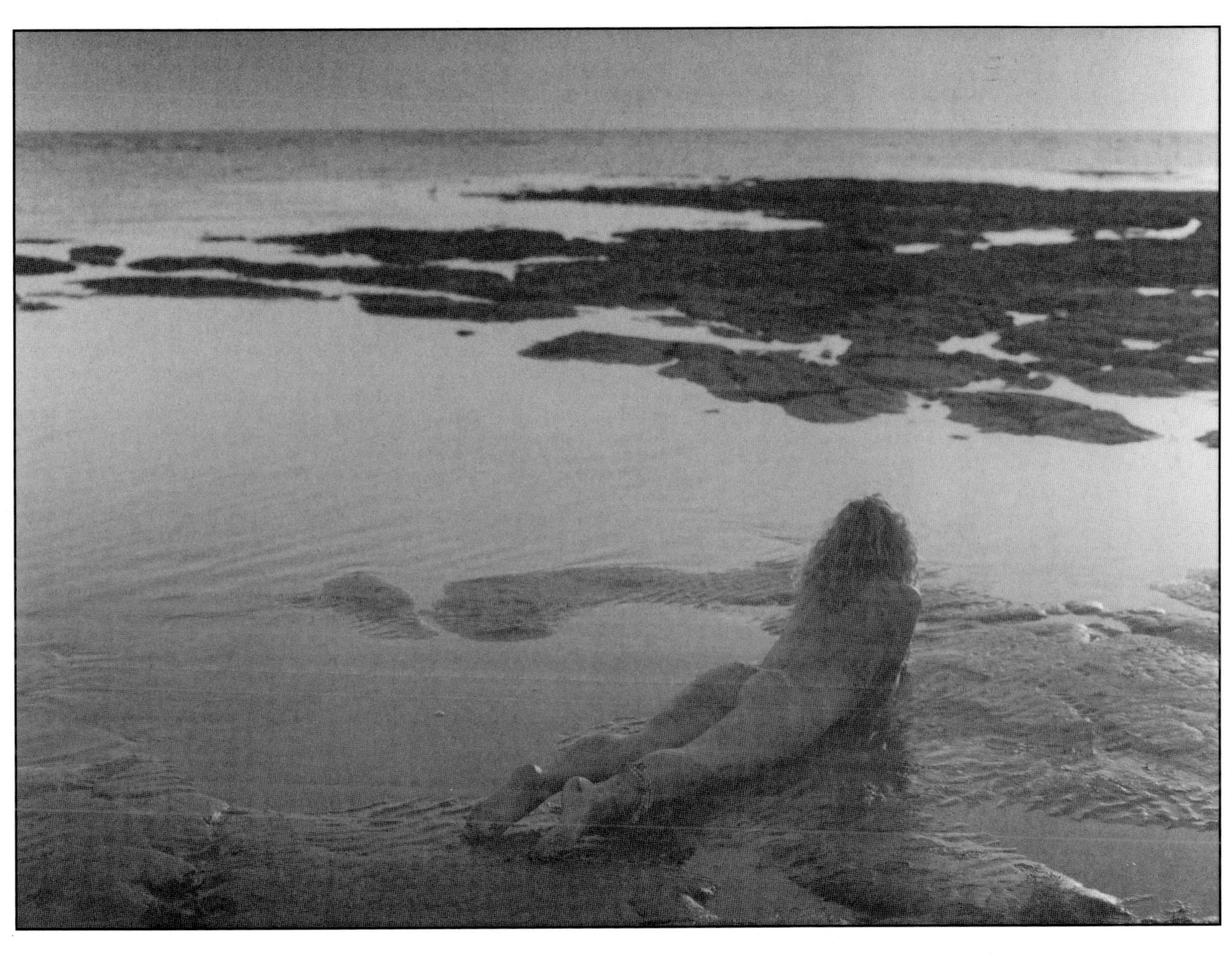

plate 47

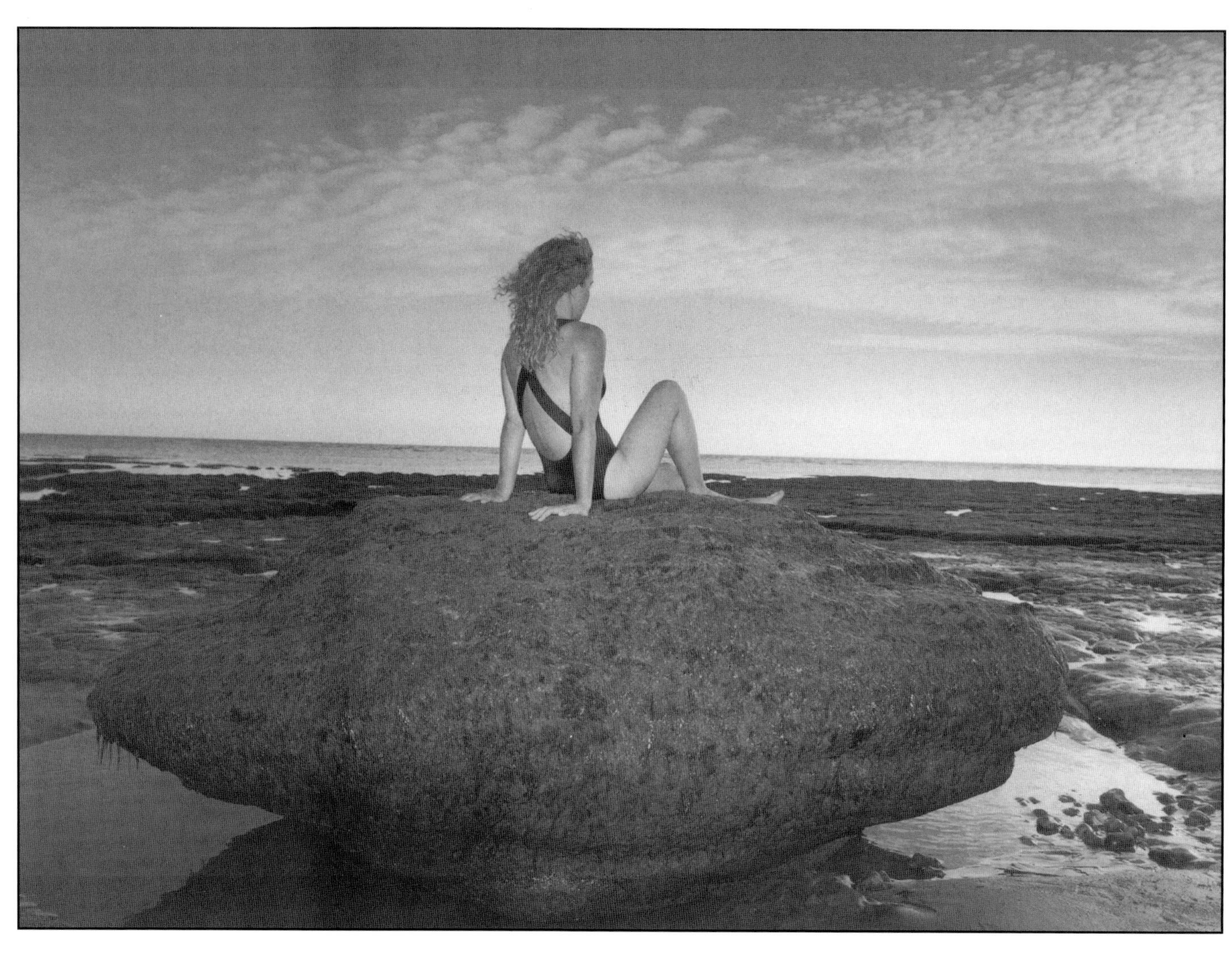

plate 48

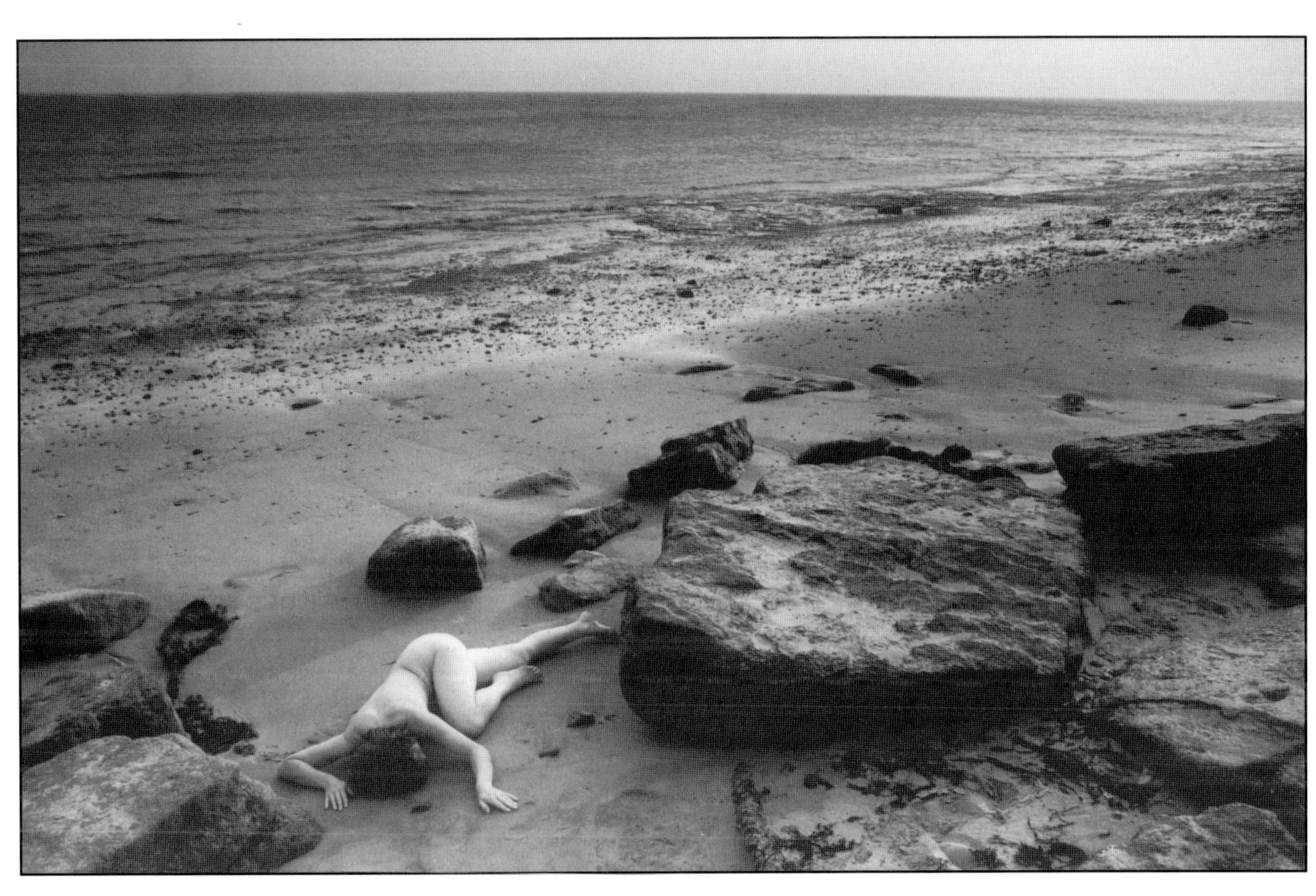

plate 49

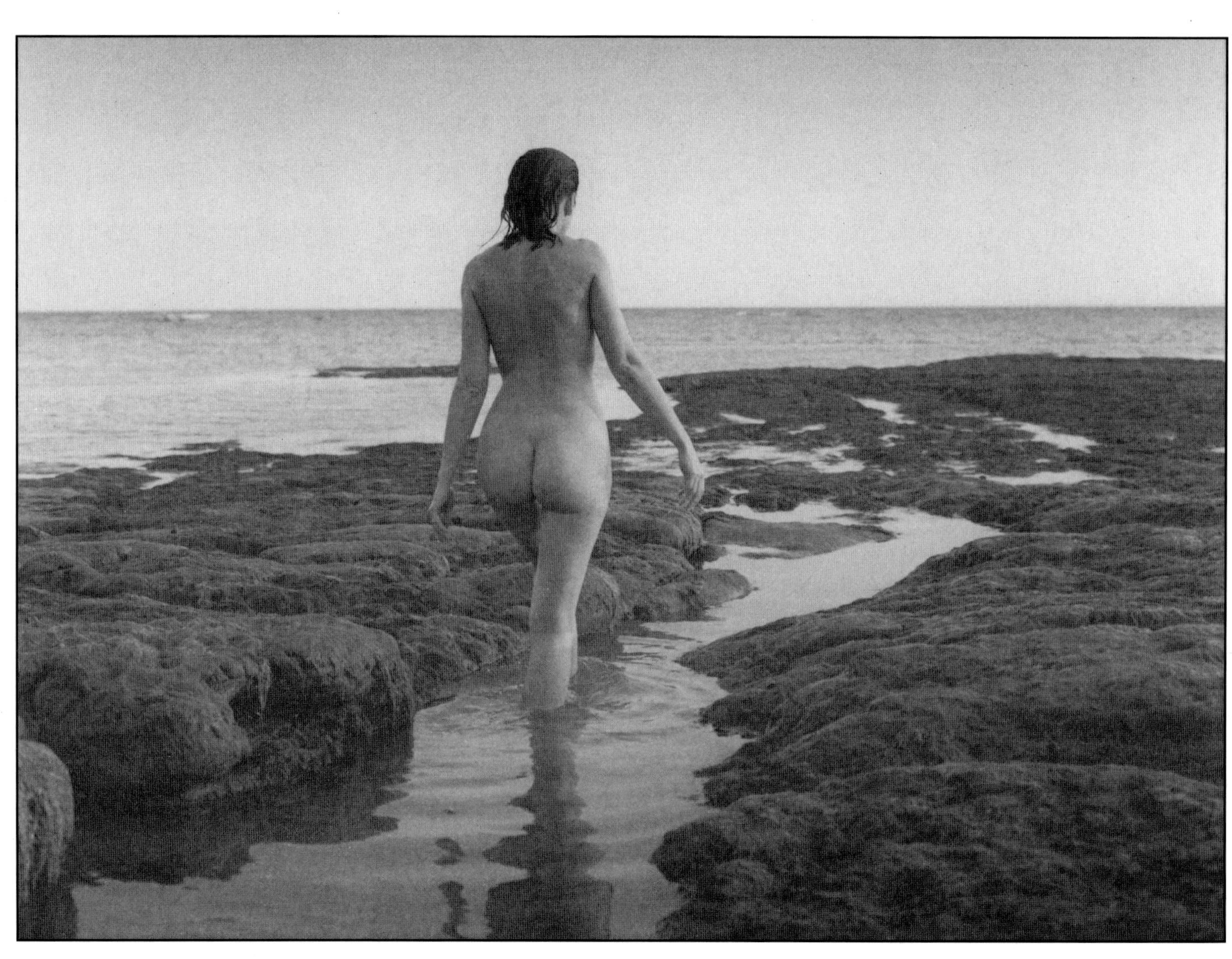

plate 50

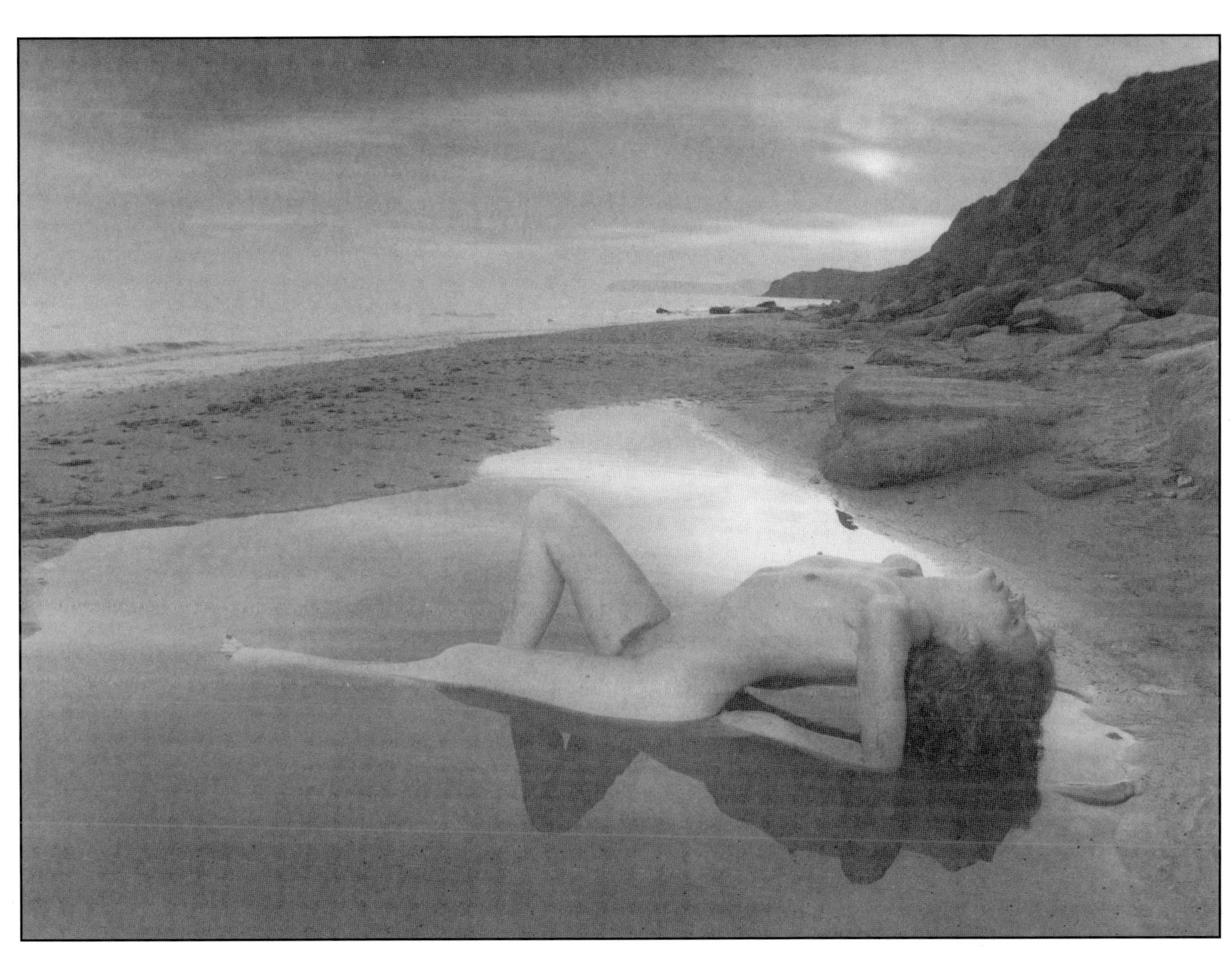

plate 51

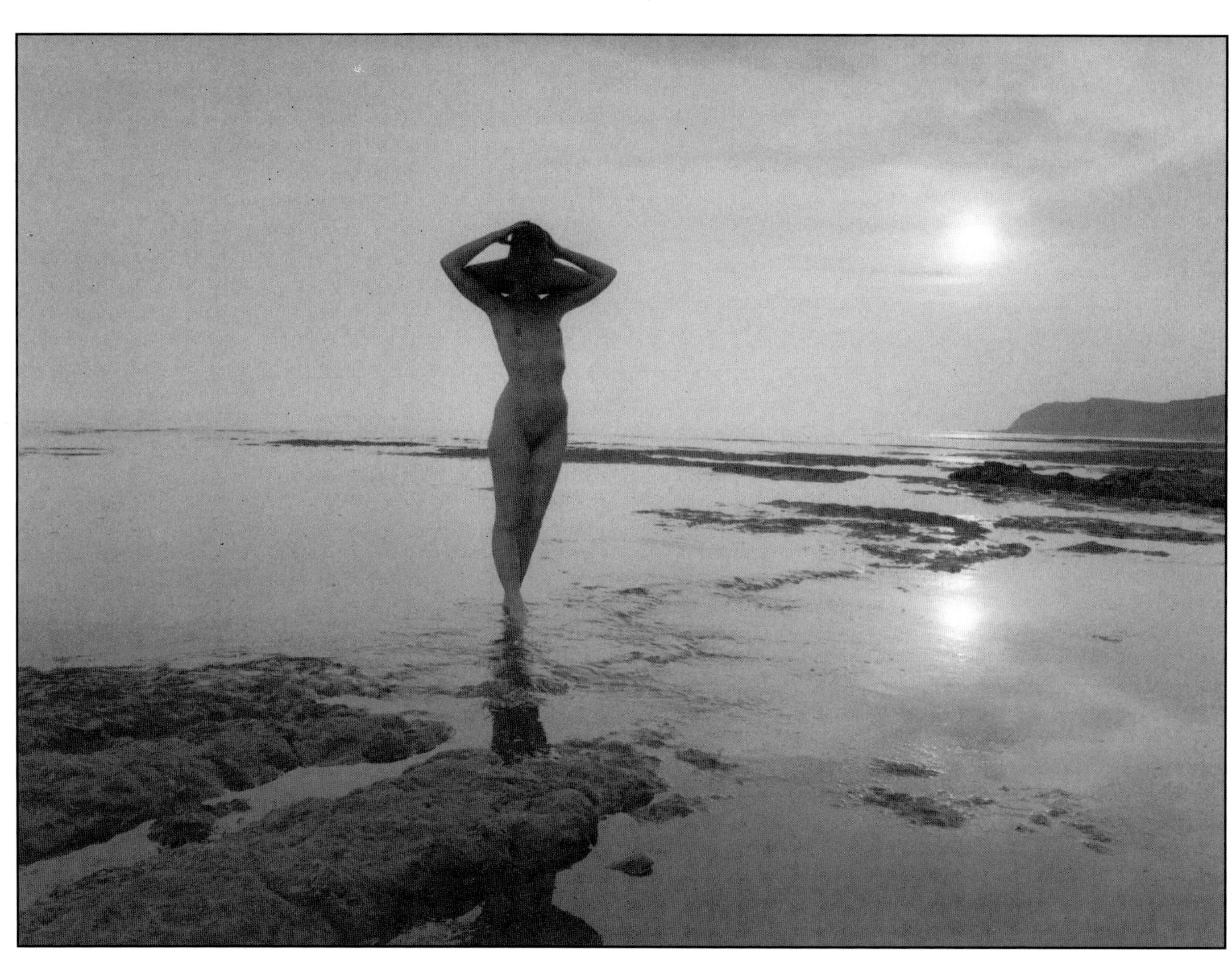

plate 52

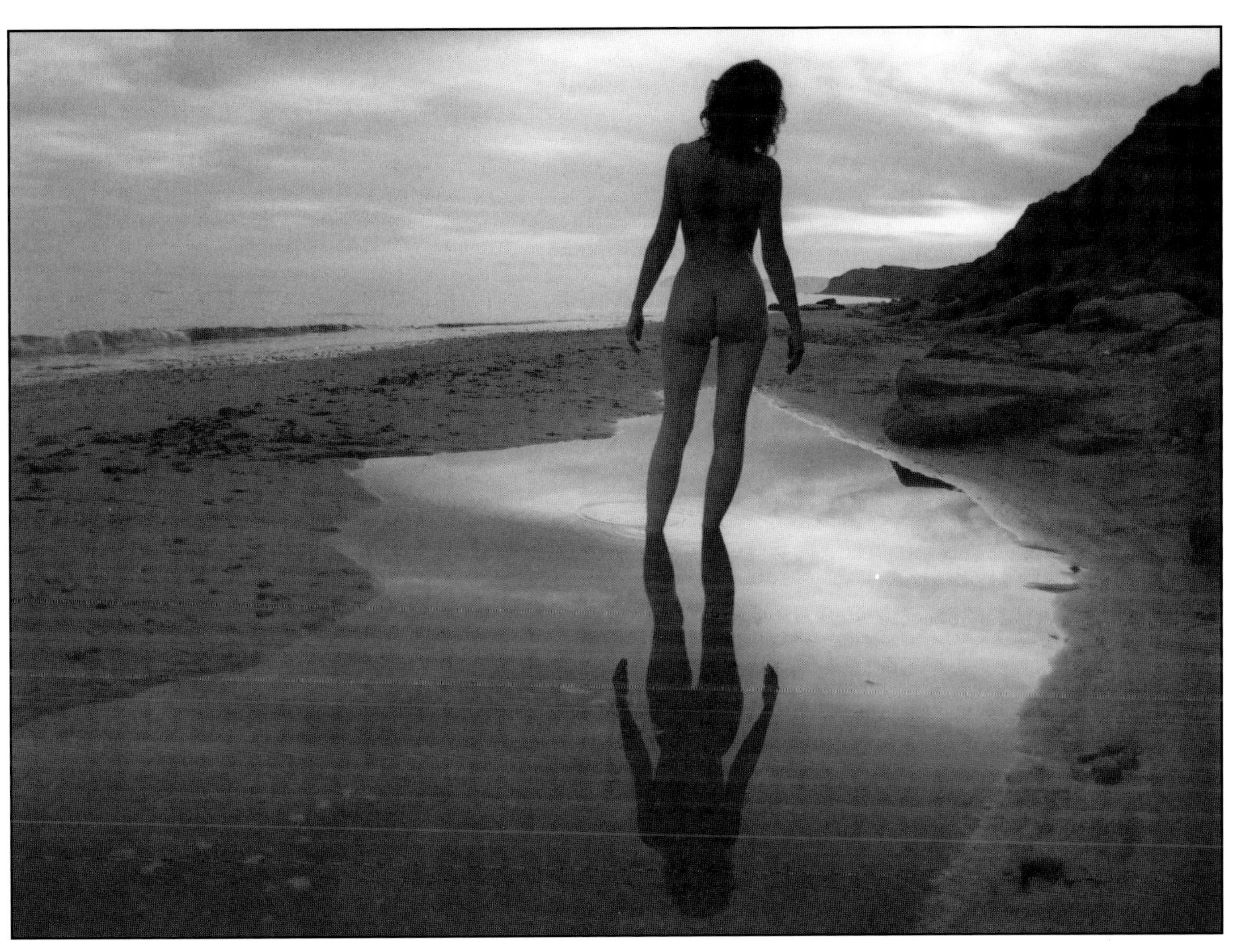

plate 53

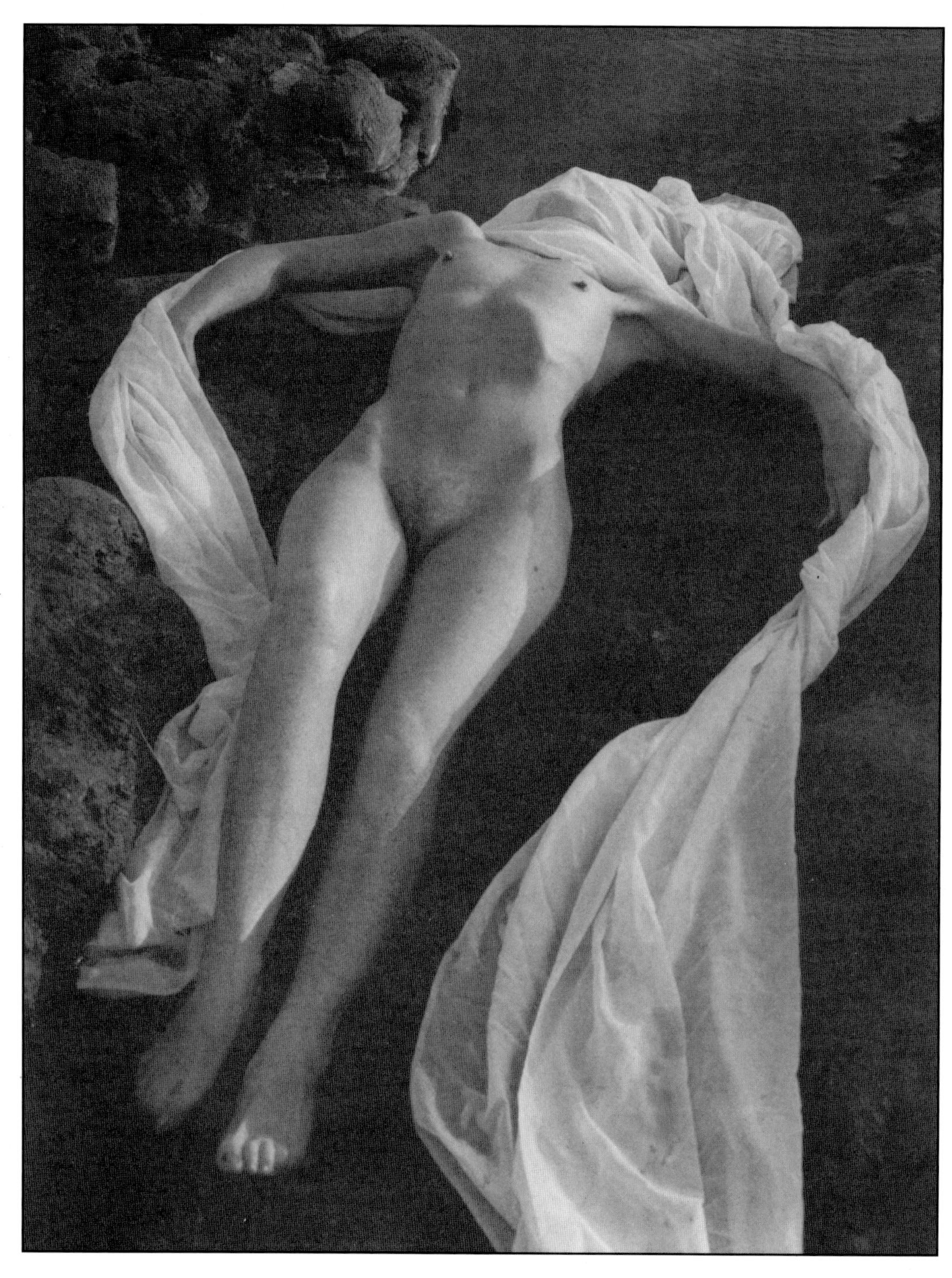

plate 54

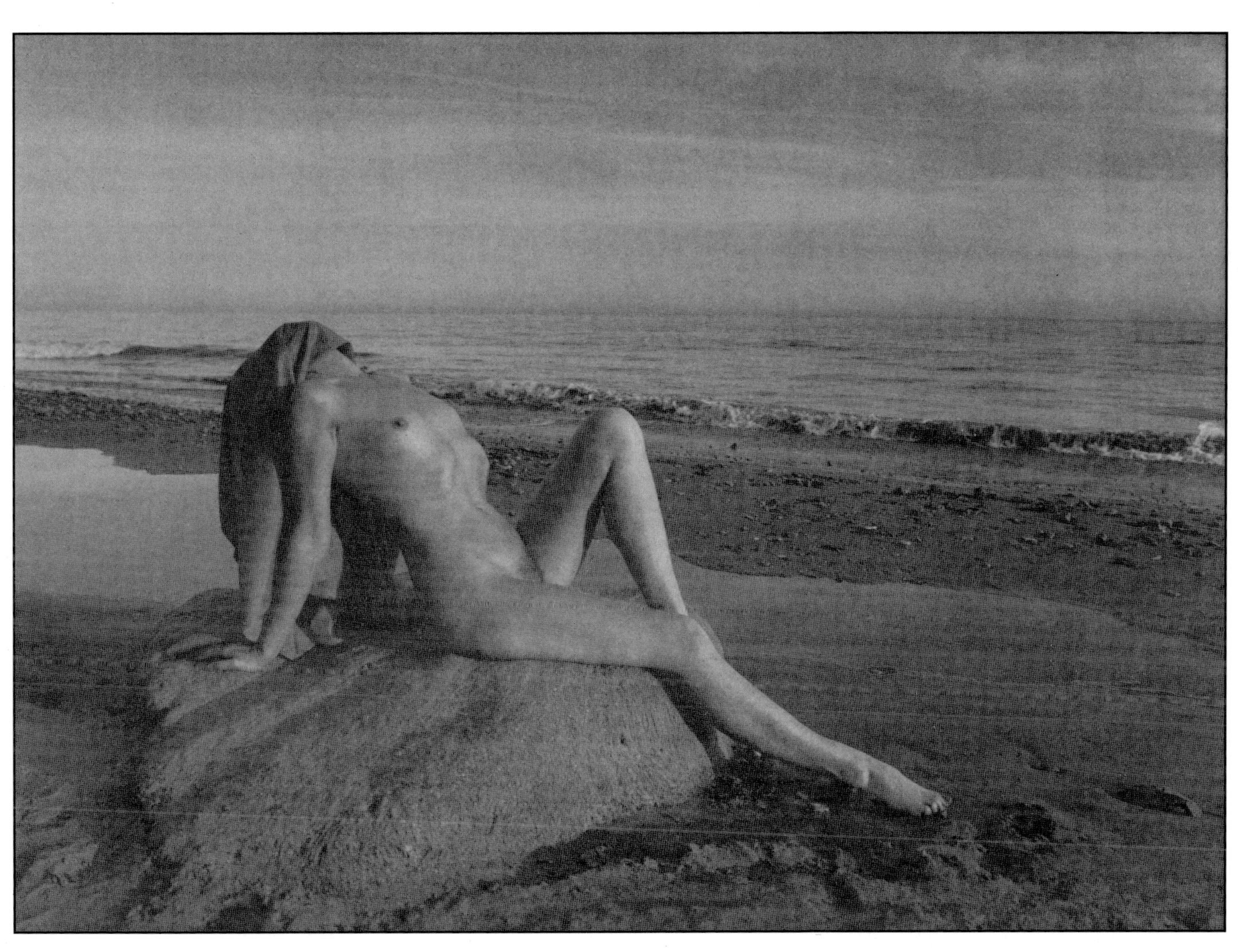

plate 55

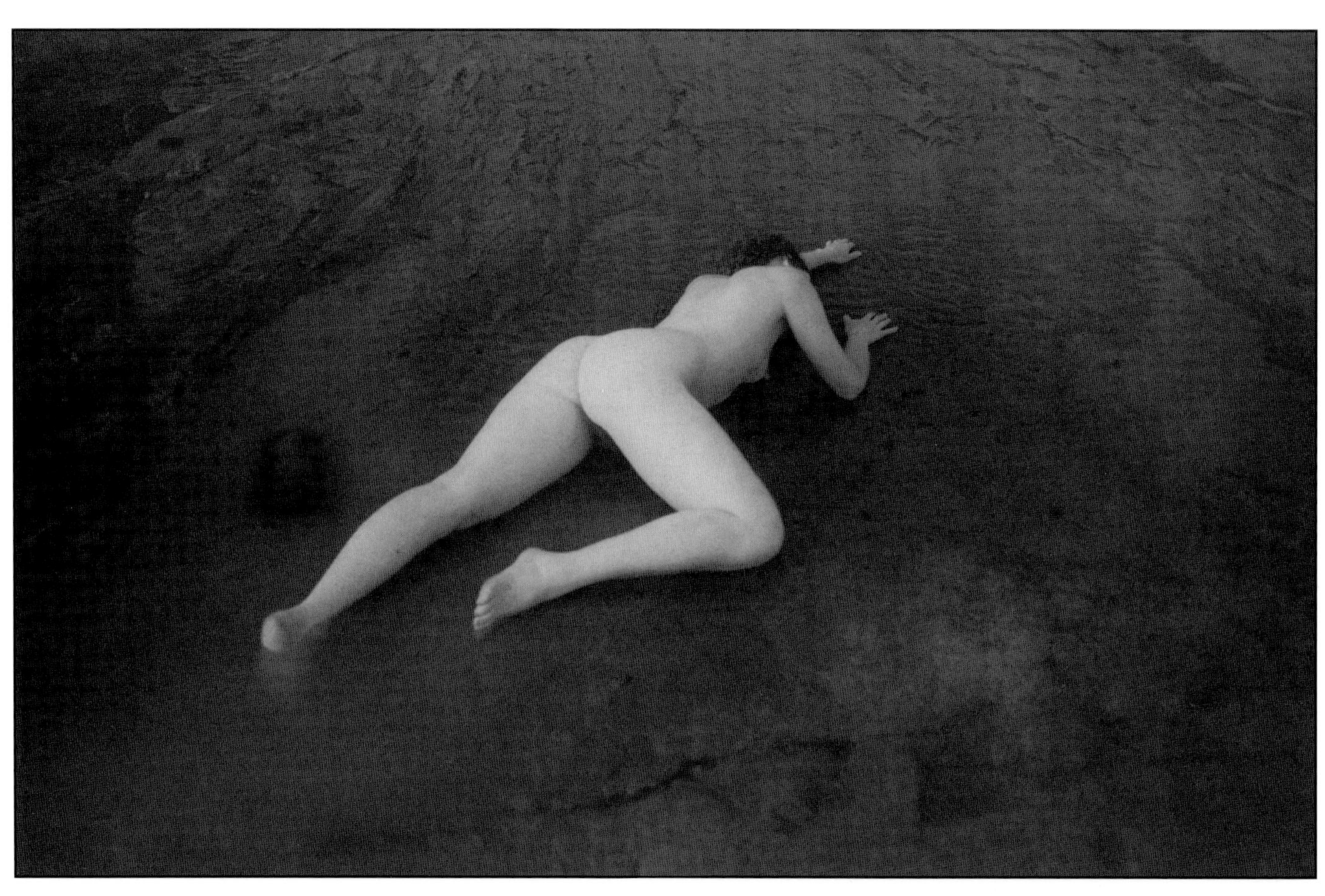

plate 56

60

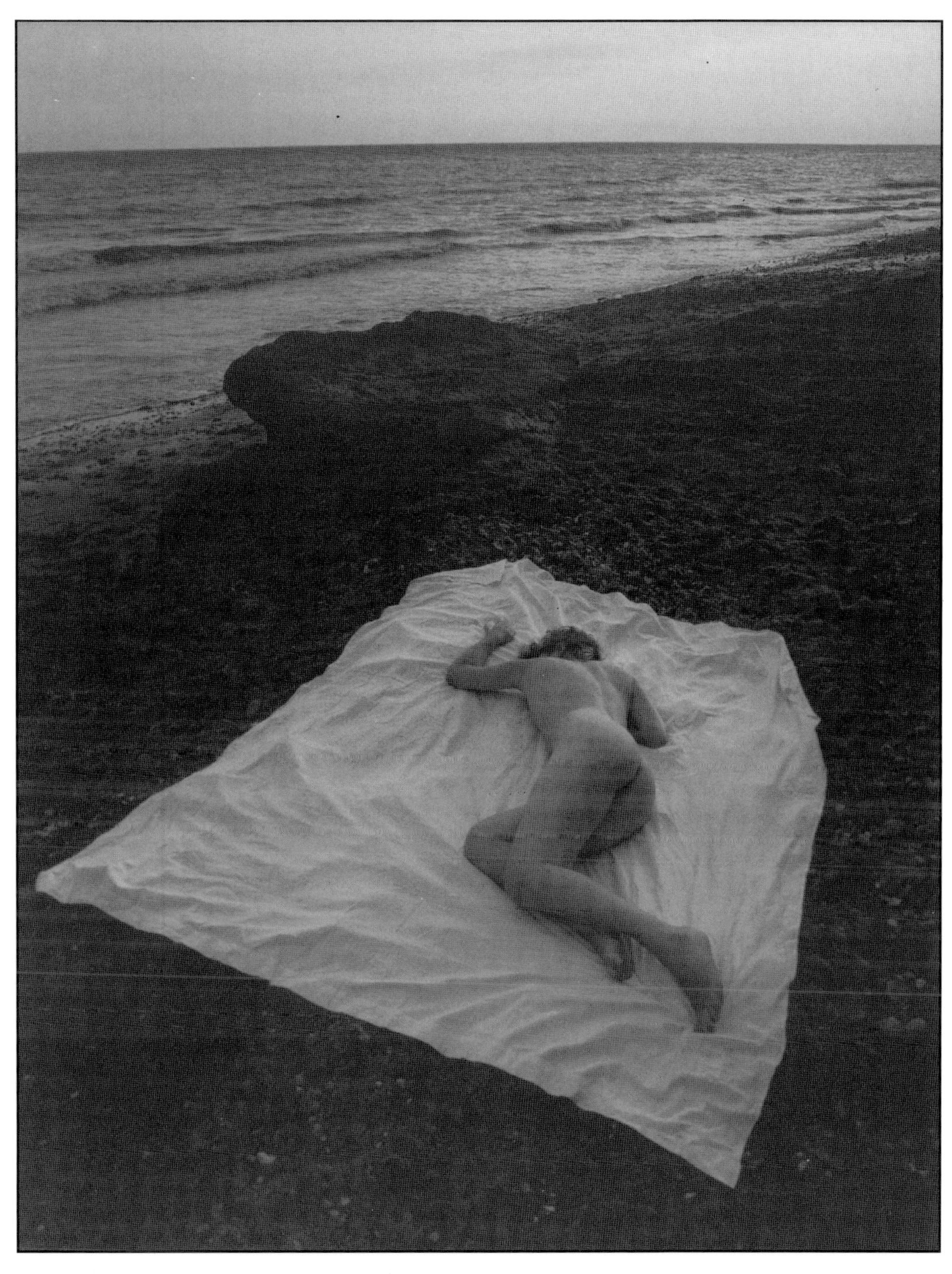

plate 57

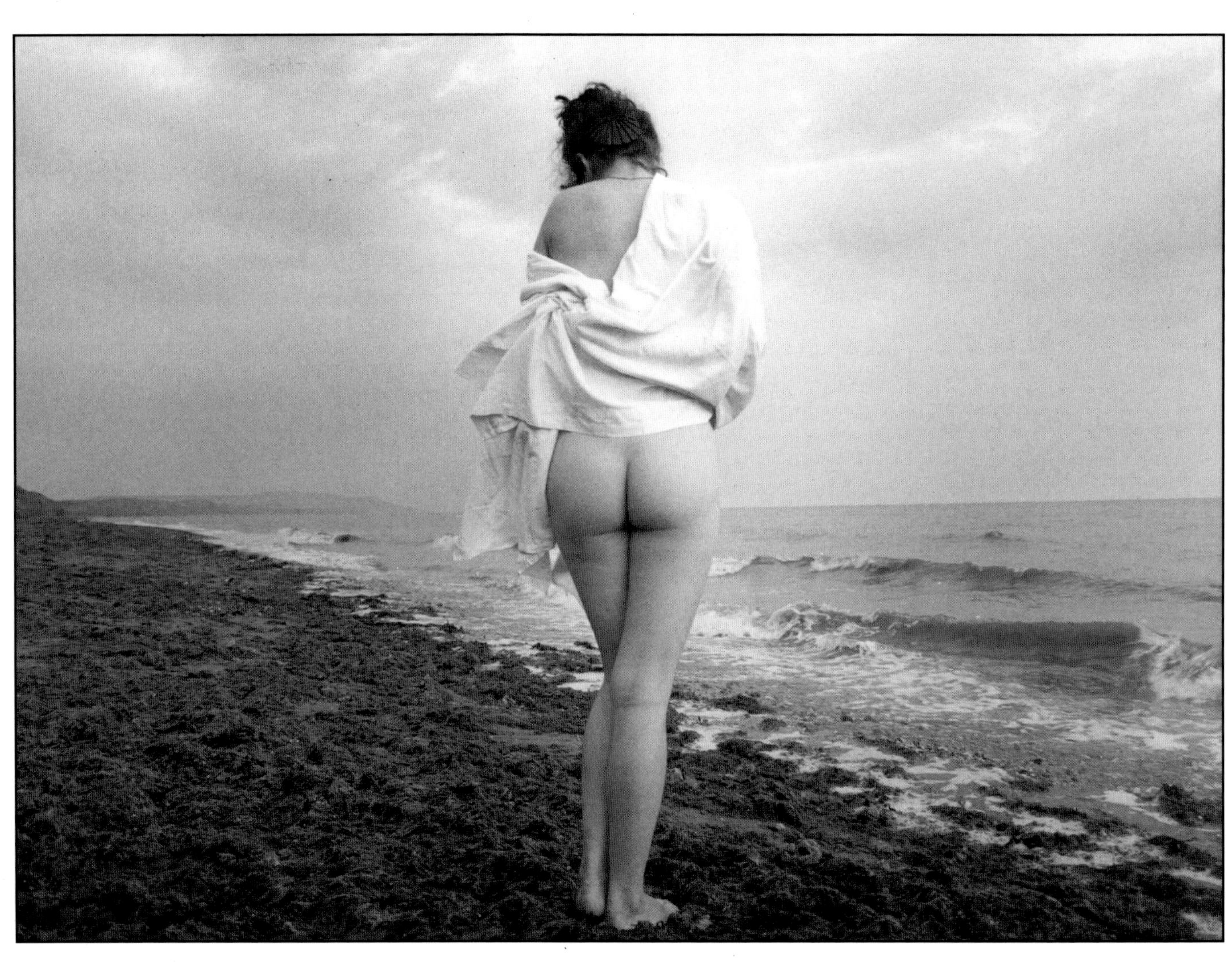

plate 58

Friends of Creative Monochrome is a supporters' group for all those who share the enthusiasm to see high quality monochrome photography reach the widest possible audience through our publishing programme. For our current catalogue and details of membership of Friends of Creative Monochrome please write to:

Creative Monochrome Limited,
20 St Peters Road, Croydon, Surrey, CR0 1HD
or telephone 0181 686 3282 or fax 0181 681 0662